DYING WORDS

To Rev-Ellen + Steven — with great affection.

DYING WORDS

The AIDS Reporting
of Jeff Schmalz

And How It Transformed
The New York Times

SAMUEL G. FREEDMAN

with

KERRY DONAHUE

CUNY JOURNALISM PRESS
The City University of New York

CUNY JOURNALISM PRESS IS THE ACADEMIC IMPRINT OF THE CUNY GRADUATE
SCHOOL OF JOURNALISM, PART OF THE CITY UNIVERSITY OF NEW YORK
219 WEST 40TH STREET, NEW YORK, NY 10018
WWW.PRESS.JOURNALISM.CUNY.EDU

© 2015 Samuel G. Freedman and Kerry Donahue

All rights reserved. No part of this book may be reproduced or transmitted in any form or by any means, electronic or mechanical, including photocopy, recording, or any information storage retrieval system, without permission in writing from the publisher, except brief passages for review purposes.

First printing 2015

Cataloging-in-Publication data is available from the Library of Congress.
A catalog record for this book is available from the British Library.

ISBN 978-1-68219-036-4 paperback
ISBN 978-1-68219-037-1 e-book

Typeset by AarkMany Media, Chennai, India. Printed by BookMobile in the United States and CPI Books Ltd in the United Kingdom.
The U.S. printed edition of this book comes on Forest Stewardship Council-certified, 30% recycled paper.

ALSO BY SAMUEL G. FREEDMAN

SMALL VICTORIES
THE REAL WORLD OF A TEACHER, HER STUDENTS, AND THEIR HIGH SCHOOL

UPON THIS ROCK
THE MIRACLES OF A BLACK CHURCH

THE INHERITANCE
HOW THREE FAMILIES AND AMERICA MOVED FROM ROOSEVELT TO REAGAN AND BEYOND

JEW VS. JEW
THE STRUGGLE FOR THE SOUL OF AMERICAN JEWRY

WHO SHE WAS
MY SEARCH FOR MY MOTHER'S LIFE

LETTERS TO A YOUNG JOURNALIST

BREAKING THE LINE
THE SEASON IN BLACK COLLEGE FOOTBALL THAT TRANSFORMED THE SPORT AND CHANGED THE COURSE OF CIVIL RIGHTS

To the Mishpacha
Who remembered and who trusted

CONTENTS

- 1   THE INTERVIEWEES
- 5   A NOTE ON METHODS AND SOURCES
- 7   FOREWORD

- 17   PART ONE: PRODIGY
- 63   PART TWO: CRACKED WIDE OPEN
- 121   PART THREE: LEGACY

- 163   AFTERWORD
- 167   GAYS IN JOURNALISM DURING THE AIDS YEARS: A TIMELINE
- 169   JEFF SCHMALZ COVERING AIDS: A SELECTED BIBLIOGRAPHY
- 171   INDEX
- 175   ACKNOWLEDGMENTS
- 183   THE AUTHORS

THE INTERVIEWEES

Soma Golden Behr was national editor of *The Times* from 1987 to 1993, when she became assistant managing editor.

Bill Clinton was president of the United States from 1992 to 2000.

David Dunlap has been a reporter and editor for *The New York Times* since 1976.

Mary Fisher is an author, artist, speaker, and philanthropist who advocates for people who are HIV-positive, as she is.

Max Frankel was executive editor of *The New York Times* from 1987 to 1994.

Earvin (Magic) Johnson, a championship basketball player in the NCAA and NBA, is an entrepreneur and a philanthropist and activist on issues including HIV/AIDS.

Elizabeth Kolbert, winner of the 2015 Pulitzer Pride for General Non-fiction, is a staff writer for *The New Yorker,* specializing in the environment. She was previously a reporter for *The Times.*

Larry Kramer, an award-winning playwright and Oscar-nominated film producer, was a founder of Gay Men's Health Crisis and ACT UP.

Joseph Lelyveld was managing editor of *The Times* from 1990 to 1994, when he became executive editor.

Eric Marcus is the author of books including *Making Gay History: The Half-Century Fight for Lesbian & Gay Equal Rights*.

Richard Meislin was a reporter, foreign correspondent, and editor for *The Times* from 1976 until 2015.

Adam Moss was editorial director and then editor of *The New York Times Magazine* from 1993 to 2004, when he left to become editor of *New York* magazine.

Adam Nagourney covered politics for *The Daily News* and *USA Today* before joining *The Times* as a national correspondent. He is the co-author with Dudley Clendinen of *Out for Good: The Struggle to Build a Gay Rights Movement*.

Michael Norman was a reporter and columnist for *The Times*. With his wife, Elizabeth Norman, he is the co-author of the best-selling *Tears in the Darkness: The Story of the Bataan Death March*.

Anna Quindlen was a reporter, editor, and columnist for *The Times* before becoming a best-selling novelist.

Randy Shilts was the author of *And the Band Played On*, a widely-acclaimed history of the early years of the AIDS epidemic.

Allan Siegal was news editor of *The Times*.

Michael Specter is a staff writer, specializing in science, for *The New Yorker*. He previously covered AIDS for *The Washington Post* and was a news assistant on *The Times*.

Thomas Stoddard was a lawyer and activist on issues of gay rights with the Lambda Legal Defense Fund.

Arthur Sulzberger, Jr. is publisher of *The Times*.

Michael Wilde, an editor, is Jeff Schmalz's brother-in-law.

Wendy Schmalz Wilde, a literary agent, is Jeff Schmalz's sister.

A NOTE ON METHODS AND SOURCES

All of the direct quotations in this book are drawn from the authors' interviews, with the following exceptions. The interviews with Bill Clinton, Earvin (Magic) Johnson, Larry Kramer, Randy Shilts, and Thomas Stoddard are from the original recordings made by Jeff Schmalz. The interview with Max Frankel, the Q&A with Dalton School students, and the exchange between Forrest Sawyer and Jeff Schmalz are from video recordings made by ABC for its *Day One* news-magazine show. The eulogies for Jeff Schmalz are from a recording made for Wendy Schmalz Wilde of the memorial service at the Dalton School. Michael Wilde provided the original text of his diary. In all of the above cases, the authors have lightly edited the transcribed interviews for the sake of clarity.

FOREWORD

Midway through June of 1982, I was summoned from my usual post in the Connecticut bureau of *The New York Times* to spend two weeks doing a night shift in the legendary newsroom on West 43rd Street in Manhattan. I was 26 and less than a year into working at *The Times*, my dream job, one I had coveted since first visiting *the Times* on a sixth-grade class trip. I was also in the midst of some struggle, trying to rapidly raise my standards from the local newspapers of my career thus far to the rarefied echelon of the *Times*.

The temporary reassignment had been orchestrated by my immediate superior, Jeff Schmalz. While Jeff was only two years older than me, he had worked at *The Times* since his late teens and dropped out of Columbia University at barely 20 to become a full-time copy editor. Jeff's official title was regional editor, the person charged with overseeing *The Times*' suburban coverage, though he essentially ran the city desk. The honorific Jeff really deserved with me was "rabbi," newsroom slang for that kind of boss who guided and guarded you. Even if the night shift sounded like a punishment, Jeff saw it as a way for me to get to know more editors and them to get to know me.

As the last day of my two-week stint approached, Jeff gave me a field assignment. I would cover the Gay Pride Parade. I understood his agenda right away. Already in my brief time on *The Times*, Jeff had told me he was gay, the first person in my life to make what was then a risky admission. Somehow, in spite of my overall ignorance, he'd sized me up as someone capable of being sensitized to the reality of gay existence and of doing some small part to personally improve *The Times*' coverage of it.

Walking along the parade route in Greenwich Village, trawling for a vivid scene or pithy quote, I spotted a young man named Jeff Natter. We knew each other from high school in Highland Park, N.J.; a year younger than me, Natter had succeeded me as editor of the school paper. He had also been the unrequited crush of my sister's best friend. I had heard that he was working as an actor, but now as I reintroduced myself, he stood along Fifth Avenue wearing a hat emblazoned with the motto, "An Army of Lovers Can Not Fail."

I put that detail, and Jeff Natter's name, in my article. He called me a few days later to say that, through the vehicle of *The New York Times*, he had come out to his parents. It occurred to me that in some sense I was outing Jeff Schmalz, as well—not in the sense of revealing the gay identity that he kept secret from his newsroom superiors but in the sense of doing some small good deed on behalf of tolerance in a largely intolerant time and place. Jeff burned for *The Times* to cover gay people and issues in a way that wasn't exotic or judgmental, and he knew the newsroom politics well enough to recognize that such change would not happen easily. Young, straight, sympathetic reporters like me were Jeff's stealthy emissaries. After all, these were the days when official *Times* style forbade using the word "gay" except as part of a direct quote. The only acceptable term otherwise was "homosexual," so chilly and clinical and alien. (Indeed, the headline that editors put on my story was "Pride and Joy at Homosexual Parade.") I was just beginning to grasp the fear that many gay and lesbian journalists on *The Times* felt, a force that kept many in the closet and compelled several into paper marriages for the sake of their careers.

Jeff must have first told me he was gay during one of our periodic working lunches. I can't remember the exact time and place, or the precise words he used. But I remember his tone: calm, confident, matter-of-fact. Nothing had prepared me for the liberating ordinariness of his disclosure. My greatest mentor, a high school English teacher named Robert W. Stevens, had been a gay man driven into alcoholism by the pressure of being closeted in our small New Jersey town. When a college classmate of mine in the late 1970s confided to a group of friends that he had a gay brother, we took the news with a somber hush, as if to commiserate over a birth defect or deformity. And yet I considered myself an enlightened, liberal guy.

Then, not so many years later, here was Jeff Schmalz steering my path at *The Times*. If I had done well on an assignment, the phone rang for me in the Connecticut bureau, and Jeff would crisply say, "Hey, Scoop." Jeff taught me that when I had intrinsically dramatic material I should keep my tone sober and subdued—"dead-away" was his phrase for it. He policed my copy to ensure that my own biases never showed through. "Without fear or favor" was *The Times'* mantra; "straight down the middle" was Jeff's mandate to me. And when I faltered—I can recall one particular article about a nuclear-freeze referendum in a Connecticut town – then the phone rang in the bureau with a different greeting. "When I read this story," Jeff would say icily, "I know exactly what Sam Freedman thinks." I would rewrite as quickly as possible to regain Jeff's approval.

In some disconcerting ways, too, Jeff struck me as a pure product of *The Times*, a company man. In one of my first feature stories for the paper, about a hockey league for investment bankers and corporate lawyers in the tony suburb of New Canaan, I described a player changing out of his Paul Stewart shirt. "If you're going to write for *The New York Times*," Jeff told me with both levity and edge as he edited the piece, "you're going to have to know how to spell Paul Stuart." A few months later, during a worrisome dry spell for me, Jeff assigned me to profile the former Supreme Court Justice Potter Stewart on his return to his alma mater, Yale University. The article got big, splashy display, and I was grateful and relieved. I told Jeff as much during a subsequent lunch. But I also told him that there were plenty of people who went to public universities like Rutgers and UConn who were also *Times* readers, and stories about those schools also deserved attention, too. Jeff was unswayed. "When you read *The New York Times*," he replied, "you expect to see a Tiffany's ad and you expect to see a story about Yale."

Jeff's lessons and advocacy ultimately brought me such visibility within *The Times* that I was plucked from Connecticut to cover the Broadway theater beat, a plum assignment. I wound up renting an apartment on the Upper West Side a few blocks from Jeff's, so I saw him more both at work and outside the office. In our conversations, he offered me a window into a gay life that was neither tormented nor apologetic. When we had dinner after deadline one night at a Theater District bar Jeff favored, he flirted with the host right in front of me. He talked about the gay clubs he frequented, the way the dance floor lit up when all the chorus boys showed up after their Broadway shows. He even joked about his taste in men. "Twinkies," he explained. "Young, blond, and dumb."

Jeff also confided an unexpected bit of self-doubt to me. He wanted to move into reporting from editing, and he worried aloud that he had so thoroughly mastered the quintessential *New York Times* story that he would never be able to break out of the formula. He would never have a voice of his own. Here was another way of being a company man; here was another sort of being closeted. And I had to admit Jeff's fears were well founded. When he began covering Connecticut in 1983, taking over what had been my beat, his articles seemed to me flawlessly constructed, impeccably reported, and yet ineffably mechanical.

On a day-to-day basis, our paths diverged in 1987, when I left *The Times* to start writing books. Jeff was rising up the ladder to become bureau chief in Albany and then Miami. From afar, I followed his in-print feud with Governor Mario Cuomo, which started to loosen up something in Jeff's prose. He was brought back to New York as deputy national editor, a sure sign he was on the trajectory to become one of the top editors on the paper.

Then, in December 1990, I heard that Jeff had collapsed in the newsroom. Soon after, I learned that he had been diagnosed with AIDS. Remarkably, in that era before drug cocktails to manage the disease, Jeff recovered enough to return to work. And during the last year of his life, he took on the AIDS beat, finding his own voice after years of enabling the voices of reporters whom he mentored. His profiles of basketball star Magic Johnson and activists Mary Fisher and Tom Stoddard, among many other people with HIV or AIDS, were filled with not only Jeff's characteristic intelligence but an empathy and heart that were new in his copy. The disease that would kill Jeff cracked his soul wide open; his murderer provoked his greatest work.

The last time I saw Jeff was in the autumn of 1993. He lay dazed and mute in his bedroom, far gone with AIDS. On his nightstand, I saw the paperback book he'd evidently been reading, *Of Mice and Men*. Something about Steinbeck reminded me of another detail from my conversations with Jeff. For all of his Manhattan panache, the crisply pressed trousers and shirt, the impeccable navy blazer, he spoke tenderly about having grown up in a small Pennsylvania town.

For recreation, his mother sometimes took him to watch the volunteer firefighters battling a blaze. Someday, Jeff told me, he wanted to write a novel about all that.

Jeff died on November 6, 1993, at the age of 39. On a strangely glistening night several weeks later, I went to his favorite restaurant, Chanterelle, for a private memorial service that somehow, in an unforced way, became a festive celebration of his life. I knew from Jeff that his sister, Wendy, his only sibling, was a literary agent. I introduced myself to her that night, and I told her how honored I was to have been invited. I asked her how she had chosen the guests. "This was supposed to be Jeff's 40th birthday party," she explained. "He'd made up the list."

Death was Jeff's final lesson to me. Just as he was the first openly gay man I knew, he was the first person I knew to die of AIDS. In the years since then, his absence has harrowed me. I could not separate the upward arc of my writing career from the ways Jeff had elevated my abilities and negotiated my way through the labyrinth of *Times* newsroom politics, which had ruined people far more talented than me. For lack of a better term, I felt survivor guilt. And beyond it, I grieved that as the years passed, fewer people would remember who Jeff Schmalz was and what tremendous work he had done.

Indeed, one evening nearly 20 years after Jeff's death, my fiancée and I were having dinner with another couple—she a screenwriter, he a former magazine journalist now working on a cable series about journalism. The conversation turned to New York State's recent

FOREWORD • 13

legalization of same-sex marriage, a stance vociferously endorsed by *The New York Times*. I mentioned how remarkable it was to me, having lived through such a homophobic period on the paper, to see *The Times* become a champion of gay rights. Then I found myself talking about Jeff and his AIDS articles, fully expecting that my friends would be familiar with him and them. But they drew a blank.

That blank, of course, made sad sense. Jeff had been dead for a generation. Newspaper writing is evanescent, as perishable as the paper it is printed upon. Still, I could not believe that people who would know the names and work of Randy Shilts, Larry Kramer, Tony Kushner, Terrence McNally, Michelangelo Signorile, Andrew Sullivan—those artists and journalists who bore witness to the AIDS plague – could not know of Jeff Schmalz. It felt like a moral duty for me to do something to rescue Jeff from obscurity.

Those friends at dinner suggested a film, but I am no filmmaker. They suggested writing a biography, but I believed Jeff had left his own written record. As months passed, what came to me was the sound of voices—the voices of those who had known and worked with Jeff, the voices of those whom he had interviewed, the voice of Jeff himself. The story of Jeff Schmalz, it seemed to me, wanted to be a radio documentary. And in book form it wanted to be an oral history.

I went to see Wendy Schmalz Wilde, to ask for her blessing. She gave me that, and she gave me more: a set of micro-cassettes on which Jeff had recorded his AIDS interviews. I also went to see Arthur Sulzberger, Jr., Jeff's friend and the publisher of *The New*

York Times. I sought both institutional and personal support—not because the documentary and oral history will be authorized, sanitized accounts of Jeff's years at The Times, but precisely because the newspaper must be shown with its flaws in how it reported on gay issues and how it treated its own gay staff members.

Although I continue to maintain a formal association with The New York Times, writing a monthly column on religion, the content of this book and the companion radio documentary were produced by me and my collaborator, Kerry Donahue, with complete editorial independence.

We began with a clear, linear goal: to recount Jeff Schmalz's life and work in his years on The Times. As we proceeded, though, it soon grew evident that Jeff's story unfolded into larger stories: what it meant to grow up gay amid anti-gay bigotry; how wrenching it was to come out, for fear of being scorned by friends and family and ostracized or fired by employers; the blind spot in the conscience of the nation's most powerful and respected newspaper; the sheer terror and rampant death experienced by people with HIV or AIDS in the years before drug cocktails made them endurable diseases.

There can be no gainsaying the bleakness of disease, death, self-denial, and bigotry. And yet, finally, Jeff's experience tells us something essential about the positive changes in American society, including The New York Times, in the acceptance of its LGBT citizens over the past generation. Jeff Schmalz did not live to see those changes, but his life and work helped to make them possible.

PART ONE: PRODIGY

Wendy Schmalz Wilde

We grew up in a suburb of Philadelphia called Willow Grove where there was a big amusement park for years and years and years. The tagline was "Life is a lark at Willow Grove Park."

We grew up in a single-mother household. My parents split up before I was born, so Jeff was two and a half when my father completely left the picture. I mean he was completely gone. No contact whatsoever. My father was an alcoholic who pretty much drank himself to death when he was in his 50s. There's not really much to tell there. So my mother had a tough row to hoe. It was hard in the early '60s to have two children and work full-time. She worked for Sears Roebuck. She was a manager there. I think she had to be very strict with us. She always instilled in us a drive for perfection. It was very important to her.

When I was in school, I don't remember anybody else who only had one parent. It was very rare back then. I think she realized how hard that was going to be. And it was something Jeff didn't want people to know, that we had a single parent.

Jeff was a very adult little kid. I mean, he was always wise beyond his years. So he was very much the man of the house from the time he was very, very young. He was two and a half years older than me, but in a lot of ways he was like a father to me as much as an older brother. He did the school paper and he always had after-school jobs. He worked at a carnation nursery for a while. He liked that very much.

He was very protective of my mother. He was very domineering with me. He had a sense of humor but he was very serious and very focused for as long as I can remember. He was incredibly bright and he was always very, very driven—from the time he was nine or ten years old.

He absolutely wanted to reinvent himself. He didn't reinvent his own personality or his own sense of style. But he reinvented his past to a certain degree, because he wanted that to conform more with the image he was presenting to the world. It was very important to him to either go to Harvard or Columbia—Harvard because of the cachet and Columbia because it was in the city. Jeff graduated first in his class. He was valedictorian. He got a scholarship to Columbia for fatherless boys.

Part of his desire to go to New York was because he was gay. It had to have been. It wasn't easy to be a gay teenager in Willow Grove, Pennsylvania in 1970. It just wasn't. He wanted to come to the city where he would feel like he belonged, because he didn't feel like he belonged in our hometown for obvious reasons. Not just because he was gay, but he was so incredibly smart. He really was. He was frighteningly smart. He had this drive that most of our peers in high school didn't have. New York was a natural choice for him.

Anna Quindlen

I think there was an entire generation of gay men who looked at New York City the way Dorothy and her friends looked at Oz. I don't use that analogy facetiously. They thought, here is where I can go to be my authentic self. That meant reinvention, essential reinvention in terms of the way you looked, in terms of the way you lived, how you ate, the way your apartment looked, so on and so forth. I think Jeff was just part of that.

Eric Marcus

By the time Jeff was a young man, it was hardly a secret that New York and San Francisco had vibrant gay communities. And they were large enough cities that a young gay person could live openly and anonymously, which meant they didn't need to fear that word would get back to their hometowns that they were gay. So Jeff was hardly alone in his decision to move to New York.

Every major city in the United States has long been a magnet for gay people seeking to get away from the questions and prying eyes of family and neighbors. Ironically, it was the increased attention of the national press beginning in the mid-1960s that alerted gay people to the fact there were large gay communities in places like San Francisco, New York, Los Angeles, Chicago, and Miami.

In the June 26, 1964 issue of *LIFE* magazine, there's an article titled, "The 'Gay' World Takes to the City Streets." Here's one choice tidbit: "Homosexuality—and the problem it poses—exists all over the U.S. but is most evident in New York, Chicago, Los Angeles, San Francisco, New Orleans, and Miami. These large cities offer established homosexual societies to join, plenty of opportunities to meet other homosexuals on the streets, in bars or at parties in private homes, and, for those who seek it, complete anonymity. Here tolerance, even acceptance by the 'straight' world, is more prevalent than in smaller communities. Where the 'gay' world flourishes and presents so many social compensations, even the persistent pressure of antihomosexual police operations can be endured."

Can you imagine being an 18-year-old gay kid in Altoona, Pennsylvania, or Mobile, Alabama, or Fargo, North Dakota, and reading that article? You're on the next bus out of town heading for New York, New Orleans, or San Francisco.

Wendy Schmalz Wilde

I was the first one in the family Jeff came out to. I was 19, so he was 21 or 22. We never talked about it, but I had suspected he was gay for a long time—he never had girlfriends, he wasn't interested in sports, all the stereotypical things. He wasn't feminine, but he was this preppy, Brooks Brothers sort of guy.

One day, he said he was bringing me to a friend's apartment, but when I got there, it was clear that they were living together.

I was the one who said it. I said, "So you're gay, aren't you?" He said, "Yes." That was it. I didn't care. He was glad and I think relieved that finally somebody in the family knew about it because it's hard to be in the closet.

One thing we would talk about was that I was the late-teens and early-20s dramatic break-up girl. I would get involved with people and then when we broke up, it was always the end of the world for me. "How can I go on?" Jeff would just say, "What difference does it make? Who wants to be with somebody all the time? It's so much more interesting to be with different people all the time and just have new experiences. Get over it."

On January 22, 1973, Jeff started work at The New York Times *as a copy boy on the night shift, the bottom rung of the newsroom ladder. He had turned 19 only six weeks earlier and was in his sophomore year at Columbia University.*

Wendy Schmalz Wilde

I remember he wrote a letter to *The Times*, sort of saying, "I didn't go to private school. I don't come from a wealthy family. I'm not the sort of person you'd normally hire, but I'm terrific and you should hire me." They did. He was a copy boy and he actually dropped out of Columbia to work at *The Times*. He knew almost like a professional basketball player who'll stop at the senior year and go be a pro instead. He realized his path was at *The Times* and not in college.

Allan Siegal

These days, when you use the expression *copy boy*, people tend to wince because it sounds sexist. Except during World War II, when boys had been in short supply, *The Times* and other newspapers did not hire women to do that work, particularly on the night side, which is when the production of the paper takes place. The job is to pick things up out of one basket and deliver it to another, to take completed copy and send it in a pneumatic tube to the printers to be set in type, to take copy from reporters who were finished writing and deliver that copy to their supervising editors and ultimately from the supervising editors to the copy editors. Copy boys did miscellaneous errands. I should say that I started that way, as well, and I have vivid memories of being sent out for coffee. I can still tell you now, 70 years later, how most of those editors took their coffee, which ones wanted sugar and which ones didn't.

There were two guys named Jeff who started as copy boys at the same time. They were both, I guess you'd have to say, bushy-tailed. They were eager. They were never reluctant to do anything. They were always there before you asked for them. One of them, Jeff Ort, ultimately took up Hasidic Judaism and left the paper to live in a Hasidic community somewhere. Jeff Schmalz, of course, stayed with the paper.

He caught my eye and our eyes by being very alert to things that needed fixing. If an editor overlooked something, Jeff would tactfully bring the piece of paper back and say, "Didn't you mean to do something here?" Anytime he saw something that didn't seem to stand up to the paper's intentions, whether it was grammatical or typographical or the focus of a story or a fact missing, he said so. He understood the paper. It was as if he had been born with an innate sense of how the paper wanted to be thought of and how the paper operated. Some people never develop it. Some people work there and never develop it, but he had a real good sense of what *The Times* thought of as news, what *The Times* thought of as intelligent, grown-up language use, style, play and display of the news. And he didn't make himself obnoxious about it. Quickly it became clear that here was this kid whose job was to walk around the floor of the newsroom carrying things and delivering things and he knew what he was carrying and knew what you were doing. His suggestions were always on point.

He was eager not because he wanted to show off but because he had developed somewhere along the way a reverence for what the paper was in society and what it tried to be. He identified with that. The trick is not so much to do it as to do it without getting people riled up, without putting down the editor whom you catch in an oversight. He had that very good sense. It's rare that it happens with a copy boy. It does happen. I started out as a copy boy and I like to think I used to do it. The fact is that I became fond of Jeff because I saw a lot of myself in him.

Wendy Schmalz Wilde

Jeff was given the tear-sheet that was going to be the front page of the night before Nixon resigned. It's the huge headline that is saying "Nixon To Resign" and there's a picture of Nixon and Ford. There's a lot of blank copy and then in red, it says, "For Jeff Schmalz." He got the hot type for the headline as well. He must have done something to be worthy of getting this.

In 1975, Allan Siegal drafted Jeff to join a small team of editors in revising The New York Times Style Book *for the first time since 1962. This volume of internal rules and preferences for usage, grammar, and tone was essentially the Bible of the newsroom. And because of* The Times' *regnant position in American journalism, its* Style Book *affected the norms of many other news organizations. Just 21 years old, Jeff was being vested with responsibility far beyond his years.*

Allan Siegal

As we worked on it, we became aware that Jeff was full of suggestions. He noticed a lot of things that working editors would have liked to be able to find in their manual that were essentially gaps. He tipped us off about some things we should include. He also drafted things. I didn't realize the extent of it for a while, but eventually Lou Jordan [news editor of *The Times*, who oversaw all matters of editing and style] said to me, "We've got another editor working on this book with us." In the credits in the front of the new edition in 1976, he is credited.

In the exact words of Jordan's acknowledgment, Jeff "gave much valuable aid in research and editing, in addition to managing with sureness a manuscript containing thousands of entries." For the next dozen years, long after the 1976 edition of retitled The New York Times Manual of Style and Usage had been published, Jeff kept his own hand-marked copy of the 1962 book that he had used on the project.

Both the 1962 and 1976 editions were relevant to Jeff's life at The Times in some unintended ways, as well. The 1962 Style Book did not even list entries for "gay," "lesbian," and "homosexual," as if such people did not exist in the world The New York Times covered. The updated 1976 manual permitted use of "lesbian" as both a lowercase adjective and a capitalized proper noun as part of an organizational name. The entry for "gay" instructed as follows:

Do not use as a synonym for *homosexual* unless it appears in the formal, capitalized name of an organization or in quoted matter.

By this point in history, however, the term "homosexual" was seen by many gays and lesbians as pejorative. The Times' continued use of it was widely construed as evidence of disapproval, if not outright hostility.

Allan Siegal

As a general proposition, the generation of newsroom managers in their 60s and some perhaps in their late 50s were uncomfortable with those issues and uncomfortable with the controversy surrounding them. They preferred to have the controversial issues dealt with as oral tradition and occasionally internal memos to the copy desks. The *Style Book* has always been available to the public for sale. It was published that year by McGraw Hill and several times subsequently. I think Lou Jordan did not want to become the target of a pressure campaign in favor of any particular political issue. *Gay* wasn't the only one. [Feminists criticized *The Times* for not using the honorific *Ms.*, which like the accepted *Mr.* made no reference to a person's marital status.] They preferred to steer clear of the whole thing.

With his sexual orientation hidden and his talent abundantly visible, Jeff rose through the ranks. He became the indispensable assistant editor to two consecutive metropolitan editors, Sydney Schanberg and Peter Millones. By the early 1980s, though Jeff's official title was regional editor and his nominal bailiwick was suburban coverage, he was essentially running the entire metropolitan report.

Anna Quindlen

People talk about the essential *Times* man being arrogant, having that kind of haughty air and Jeff had that, there's no question. He did cultivate that kind of university club thing—the shirts and the shoes and the cigar and the kind of glasses that he wore. It was almost an English gentleman kind of thing.

But the essential *Times* man is also really, really smart and talented, and Jeff was so good. I first met him over the phone when he was editing my copy when I was covering the Koch Administration down at City Hall. Whenever I heard his voice on the phone, my heart sank, because I knew he was going to find the holes in the story. I just knew I wasn't anywhere near done for the night. I used to curse him deep inside. But the truth is, he just elevated the level and he loved being an important part of the greatest newspaper in the country. And he was.

Watching Jeff on the metro desk was like watching somebody play chess alone, because he would determine who he liked, who he thought was good, where he wanted them, and then he would proceed to make it happen. So if he thought somebody was really talented, it was how many moves can I make with this piece until I can get them back to New York or until I can get them a column or until I can get them out front—that kind of thing. If you were blessed by him like [William] Geist was, like Maureen [Dowd] was, it would end well for you. If you were not, you might as well be invisible.

Michael Specter

Jeff was in command. Whoever was the metro editor at the time, whether it be Syd Schanberg or Peter Millones—and they are very different types of people—they always deferred to Jeff. Jeff ran that daily report. He always had this thing, like he'd get stories that were good, but he would also get stories that were incomprehensible that he would make good. He would always come in the next morning, look at the reporter, and say the same thing, which is, "That really looked good in the paper." That was his way of not saying, "Gee, this is a great story" but also making the guy feel as good as he could. I talked to him about it and he said, "What can I say?" I don't mean this in a nasty way, but he was a really political guy and he was very savvy about using his connections in power at that institution. It was really important to do that, gay or not gay. I mean there were just factions. Years later, I covered the Kremlin and the *Times* newsroom made the Kremlin look simple.

Richard Meislin

Jeff seemed to have the genetic code of being a *New York Times* editor within him. He could instantly put together a *New York Times* package. He knew exactly what should be in a series of stories. He was amazing at taking a story that a reporter had written that was sort of so-so and spin it around to make it page one-able. He had those kinds of skills down pat.

And Jeff was really a consummate manager upwards in ways good and bad. If Jeff thought being out would have a negative effect on his career, he wouldn't do it. While Abe Rosenthal was executive editor, Jeff was seriously in the closet to anyone above him.

A.M. (Abe) Rosenthal was the brilliant and mercurial monarch of the New York Times *newsroom. A renowned foreign correspondent with a Pulitzer Prize for his coverage of Poland, he was appointed executive editor in 1977 and set about installing loyalists in many of the key leadership and middle-management positions. Rosenthal often said that he viewed his mission as keeping* The Times' *coverage "straight," by which he meant uninflected by partisan or ideological bias. His choice of adjective also functioned as an accidental yet incisive pun, conveying the tenuous situation of gay and lesbian staff members. The chilling effect, in fact, preceded Rosenthal himself and emanated from an office higher than his own.*

David Dunlap

I arrived at *The Times* in 1975 as a clerk to [James] Scotty Reston at the Washington bureau. While he was nearing the end of his career as the nation's preeminent Washington columnist, he still packed a punch. He still had so many of his long-time contacts and sources still in the administration. He was a great sort of father figure. I mean, it was just a tremendously exciting year.

When I lived in Washington, my lover from college actually took a year off from school to join me in Washington. We took an apartment together near Dupont Circle. I was certainly out to close friends, but we had as a convenient fiction a fold-out couch for when guests came by. And those included Scotty and Sally Reston. We would make probably too conspicuous a point that that was a fold-out couch. I don't think we likely fooled anyone, probably not even the Restons, but that was the cover story.

I felt completely in conflict, as if my life really were cleft and that I had my domestic life with this lovely man with whom I was in love and this professional career. I couldn't imagine reconciling the two.

I wrote to a friend of mine that year about how I yearned, having seen Reston work, for the kind of power that good journalism could confer on its practitioners but couldn't imagine how a gay man could ever know that power if revealed to be gay.

> August 7, 1975
>
> ...I am planning to travel in the deeply carpeted corridors of power, the world of somber gray suits leaning over polished oaken tables. I can taste the desire to influence the newspaper that influences the world, and by God I might yet get my turn. But is that right? Can I handle that? Is it morally right? Can I exist in both politico corporate power and homosexual affinity? . . . Can I conceal my soul and become an editorial power broker? Would that be success? . . . Might I not be happier giving it up, working on a neighborhood newspaper and letting myself embrace [my lover] in public? Can I ask [him] to abridge his life to accommodate mine? Will I lose him in my success and be forever lonely? . . . The questions... haunt me at every moment.

Richard Meislin

I came onto *The Times* as a copy boy in 1975. I was a copy boy for five weeks and then became Abe Rosenthal's news clerk. Jeff, I think, was working on a copy desk, maybe the national copy desk. We would cross paths. I knew who he was, but I wasn't even out to myself when

I came to *The Times*. And nobody at *The Times* would meet on the basis of being gay, because nobody at *The Times* in that era wanted anybody to know that they were gay.

Jeff later said he knew I was gay the first time he saw me walk across the room. I didn't know at that point. He would basically go to lunch with you or have a drink with you and would sort of do what he called "drop beads"—throw things into the conversation and see how you reacted to them. It was the kind of thing that, if you were gay, you would know what he was talking about. If you were straight, it would just pass you by. It was important to people in the newsroom, for the sake out their careers, that they not be out.

Being closeted was more a matter of omission rather than commission. There were things that you didn't say and didn't talk about. The pronoun of who you saw last weekend. You would find yourself having to laugh at the kinds of jokes where gay people were the butt of the joke. It wasn't at all uncommon. It wasn't so common that you were dealing with it everyday, but these things came up. It was the mid-'70s and people were far more comfortable about expressing themselves that way than they would be today. You either wouldn't say anything or you'd laugh along, because you had a cover to protect.

David Dunlap

My first coming-out was to Rich Meislin and it occurred in the context of the 1978 newspaper strike. I had luckily landed a contract through Paul Goldberger with Random House to take the photographs for his book, *The City Observed: New York*. I had three months to do no more than prowl Manhattan with my cameras and get to photograph all these great buildings. When it came time to do Harlem, being needlessly nervous, I asked Rich Meislin, with whom I was by that time friendly, whether he'd accompany me.

He came home with me one night after a long day's shooting and I recall fixing several rounds of what I think are now called Greyhounds—vodka and grapefruit juice. As the evening wore on, beads were dropped, as they were in those days; I recall this with so many gay men, the process of throwing out just a little bit of information to see what got picked up. If that bit was reciprocated and a little more information came from the other party, you just kept taking bolder and bolder steps. I can still picture the typical 1970s oatmeal cloth couch in my apartment. I went to the bathroom and came back out. Rich, in my absence, had situated himself on that spot on the couch where if I were to resume sitting where I had been when I left to go to the bathroom, I'd be seated right next to him. I thought, "Well, okay," and I did.

Arthur Sulzberger, Jr.

When I joined the National desk as assistant editor in the early 1980s, it was a very tough time if you were gay at *The New York Times*. You had a number of colleagues at *The Times* who quite frankly found ways of hiding the fact that they were gay, some better at it than others. Jeff was better at it, quite frankly. I'm not sure when exactly in our relationship I thought to myself, "Jeff's gay," but I think it was pretty early on. Then the question became the harder question; at what point do I say, "Is there anything you'd like to tell me, Jeff?" It was a little loaded, obviously because my dad was publisher of the paper and the executive editor, Abe Rosenthal, and he were very close.

Look, my father was one of the most decent men in the world. He was open to ideas. He was a very caring, honest man. But if there was a weakness, it was, in fact, his feelings about homosexuality. None of his children ever figured out exactly what caused that to be the case but he was. He was not as supportive of that movement as he should have been.

Joseph Lelyveld

Punch had a sort of 1950s Marine attitude to the whole thing. In fact, I think there's some question as to how much of Abe's attitude was a reflection of Punch's. Not that Punch was vicious; he was the opposite of a vicious man. But there were some things he just wouldn't listen to. I have a general sense that there was a sense that Punch was inflexible on that. Or at least nobody had ever really attempted to speak to him about it.

Allan Siegal

Some of the folklore about Abe overlooks the fact that he was not self-employed. He had a boss. Abe had a talent and a philosophy. He wanted to be viewed as the ultimate authority in that newsroom.

I think the feeling he had was that if he kept deferring to people above him, his own authority would be undercut. So he chose to pose as the final authority even on a lot of things where he was getting instructions from his boss, the publisher of the paper. Sometimes I knew which things those were and sometimes I didn't.

I can say confidently that Abe was not comfortable with homosexuality. He was not comfortable with writing about gay issues. Those were only some of the social phenomena he was not comfortable with. I don't know what in his background made him uncomfortable with it, but I do believe he had a mental picture of the readers of *The New York Times* as being, as many of them were, socially conservative, older, successful corporate officers. A lot of the time I worked for Abe, there was agitation on the staff for the paper to write in the vernacular that they used themselves, that the hip neighborhoods in the city used. I think Abe had his eye on Greenwich, Connecticut, that stratum of society where the CEOs and the college deans and the board presidents lived. And he wanted *The Times* to be welcome at their dinner tables. To some degree, he was reflecting the world that the publisher operated in. I never knew what percentage was Abe and what percentage was Abe covering for somebody else.

David Dunlap

On the spectrum of gay men at *The Times*, from most to least closeted, I would situate Jeff as being among the most closeted. Because he was, perhaps of all of us, the one who was really on a fast track. Jeff had an extraordinary sense of the politics of this place. He knew how to play *The Times* like a violin. And he combined that ability with a genuine bred-in-the-bone devotion to the standards and the power and the omniscience of *The Times*. He was the consummate *Times* man. He would have been a credible candidate for executive editor at some point. But I couldn't have imagined being openly gay and even vying for the candidacy of a senior position, which I'm sure Jeff had concluded. Although he was very active sexually and was known to those of us in the newsroom as gay, he was in a public sense absolutely in the closet.

Richard Meislin

In 1983, after I had covered the Caribbean and Central America for a year as Miami bureau chief, they asked me to become the bureau chief in Mexico. I went to Mexico City and was looking for a house while staying in a hotel. I suddenly came down with some mysterious illness that was locking up various joints in my body and causing a great deal of pain. Word got back to New York and the immediate assumption was that I had AIDS. That got to Abe Rosenthal and that was the first that he found out I was gay.

My understanding was that when I got sick, Abe called [Foreign Editor] Craig Whitney and [Deputy Foreign Editor] Barbara Crossette in. He said, "Did you know that Meislin was gay?" Craig said, "Yes." Abe said, "Did everybody know that Meislin was gay?"

Craig said, "We don't spend a lot of time talking about it, but it's not a big secret." Abe said, "Shouldn't somebody have told me?" Craig was reported to have said, "No, why?" That's the version I heard. I have no idea whether it's true or not. But that is definitely the point at which Abe found out that I was gay.

He didn't bring me back right away. I worked in Mexico for two and a half years through the Mexico City earthquake at the end of 1985, but it was widely believed that that was one of the main reasons for my coming back and not being given another foreign posting. I got brought back to metro and put on the New York Parking Violations Bureau—a scandalous story which turned out to be a great story to cover but wasn't exactly the career trajectory that I was expecting.
I would hear things from other people after my transfer back. I remember being on a plane with a correspondent from NBC, who said that they had heard from somebody in the State Department that I was too gay for *The New York Times*. Not only did that perception surprise me, but the fact that people were talking about this in the State Department certainly surprised me. It clearly carried a weight that went beyond what I thought that it did.

As it happened, my interests changed and I ended up increasingly moving into the technology of journalism rather than the reporting and editing of journalism. Who knows if that would have happened in the form that it happened if I had a traditional *New York Times* career of being a reporter and a correspondent then an editor and so on. At the moment that I was put back on metro, it was awful. It certainly felt like a punishment. I considered looking for other places to work. The fact that it was happening at least in some significant part because of my sexuality was crazy.

Anna Quindlen

In 1983, when I was six months pregnant, I became deputy metro editor. Abe Rosenthal, with whom I had a very warm relationship, took me to the Four Seasons for lunch and ordered a bottle of wine. Needless to say, he was the only one drinking the bottle of wine, since I was pregnant. About halfway through lunch, he started to talk to me about how *they* were going to try to take over the metro section and how *they* were going to try to steer me in certain directions and take certain kinds of power.

It probably took me ten to fifteen minutes to figure out that by *they*, he meant gay men. I think specifically he meant Jeff, who was assistant metro editor, who sat directly across from me on the desk and who, in a just world, would have had the promotion that went to me. I didn't even know what to say. It wouldn't have occurred to me to fight Abe on that. At some level, it seemed so crazy and out of such a clear blue sky that I wouldn't have even known how to fight back. But it became very clear to me then that Abe's homophobia was all of a piece with the Red Scare and other fears that he had of certain groups. He was an extraordinary newspaper man, but he had an incredible blind spot in that area. That day it sort of left me breathless.

What was always so odd to me was that Abe had this incredibly high opinion of some of these young men, because they were so smart and good and they were such *Times* men. Then it all evaporated the moment he found out they were gay. I wish I knew more about the psychology. I don't know whether it was garden-variety homophobia of the sort that was prevalent among men of his generation or whether there was some specific trigger for it, but it was such a powerful emotion for him. I remember when the memo went out saying that we were now going to refer to women as *Ms.* on second reference, I ran up to Abe in the newsroom and threw my arms around him and hugged him. He said, "If I had known it would have made you this happy, I would have done it years ago." He would never have had that same attitude about going to the term *gay*.

The closest thing Abe Rosenthal ever gave to an overall response to the allegations that he was homophobic and punished openly gay staff members such as Richard Meislin came many years later. In a 1992 interview with Michelangelo Signorile of The Advocate, *Rosenthal said that "people who are used to being discriminated against will sometimes take certain acts as being discriminatory when they're not."*

The controversy surrounding Rosenthal's personnel decisions may have remained primarily inside The Times. *But the newspaper's slowness in covering the emerging AIDS epidemic became an issue in the gay community nationwide. The first article by the newspaper's medical reporter, Dr. Lawrence K. Altman—"Rare*

Cancer Seen in 41 Homosexuals"—ran on page A20 next to an advertisement for the upcoming July 4 holiday in 1981. That sign of indifference to the burgeoning crisis proved typical. As David Dunlap noted in a 2014 article looking back on The Times' coverage of AIDS.

> The next article in The Times appeared in August [1981]. It was by The Associated Press. By then, more than 100 cases of Kaposi's sarcoma and pneumocystis pneumonia had been reported, overwhelmingly among gay men, almost half of whom had died. Readers waited four months for the next report, on page D24, by United Press International, as five or six new cases were appearing each week.
>
> The Times was "setting the tone for noncoverage nationally," Randy Shilts wrote in "And the Band Played On" (1987). "There was only one reason for the lack of media interest, and everybody in the [Centers for Disease Control] task force knew it: The victims were homosexuals."
>
> Not until May 25, 1983, did AIDS appear on the front page; not until 1,450 cases—558 of them ending in death — had been reported; not until the government's top health official said the investigation of AIDS would be the "No. 1 priority" of the Public Health Service . . .
>
> "Though the newspaper followed developments in the AIDS story, mention of the epidemic rarely appeared in the metro section or national news reporting," Shilts wrote.

"Homosexual reporters, particularly in New York, tended to know their place and keep their mouths shut, if they wanted to survive in the news business."

Max Frankel

I don't think *The New York Times* and maybe American society as a whole fully appreciated the plague that was upon us. And the other [factor] was that it was somehow seen as the kind of disease you don't want to touch too closely, because it dealt in the dark corners of people's lives and of homosexuals especially, who are not mainstream, and it isn't the whole society's problem. There was some of that, I think, in the attitude of all American institutions.

And then there were the difficulties. If you wanted to talk about anal intercourse, that was a phrase that some people at *The Times* found difficult to get into print. I was on the editorial page [as its editor], not in the news columns, at the time, and we used it one day, because we said, how do you describe what the danger is, how do you warn people against these things without saying that? If you just use euphemisms for all this, you're not going to educate the society. Well, that was a tough barrier for a family newspaper that wanted certain things kept out of print at the time.

Eric Marcus

The Times was viewed as this sclerotic dinosaur that was way behind the curve on gay issues before AIDS and remained behind the curve.

If you look at where *The Times* placed the 1981 article about the discovery of this new disease affecting gay men, it was way inside the newspaper. If it had been the Boy Scouts or PTA moms, it would have been on the front page. It was only in 1987 when *The Times* started using the word *gay* without quotes.

But the world in which Jeff Schmalz worked was not just *The New York Times*. He was working in the entire industry. And homophobia extended far back in terms of the newsroom. What I found when I worked in journalism during those years was a profession that was completely unprepared to deal with covering an epidemic. I should say the profession was completely unprepared to cover gay people in general, let alone an epidemic.

Randy Shilts was an award-winning journalist as a student and had come out while he was in college. He could not get a job. He wound up freelancing for a long time before he got hired by KQED television in San Francisco, which was a hard-won job. The *St. Paul Pioneer Press* ran an article with the headline, "Homo Hired to be a TV Reporter." That's in 1977.

When I went to the Columbia University Graduate School of Journalism in 1983, I was one of the only two students who came out. There was still a lot of fear around covering the AIDS crisis. I helped one of my friends do a documentary during the second semester at Columbia. We wanted to do a piece about somebody who had gotten infected with HIV at a bathhouse and we wanted to go interview him at the bathhouse. The professor said it was dangerous for us to do so.

He warned us that we could catch AIDS through the camera. I was warned by my professors at the Journalism School that I could be jeopardizing my career by being an out gay person.

That's the level at which we were operating at the time. It wasn't just that people could hardly talk about gay people. They were misinformed about AIDS in the field of journalism just as people were misinformed about gay people and AIDS everywhere.

Adam Nagourney

The way newspapers approached gay issues almost exclusively was as oddities and weirdness and stories that would make fun of that. There were two exceptions. One is when you're having gay-rights bills passed in various places and newspapers like *The New York Times* took that very seriously, because it was happening through the '70s and '80s. The other part was when AIDS began or was discovered. There was a big battle of how to control it in terms of gay bathhouses, sex clubs, and places in New York City where we knew that the virus was being transmitted. It was a big struggle going on.

You had these two narratives. One is the idea of public health and what are we going to do to control what's going on at bathhouses? And the other is gay culture being Other and deviant—not my word. Those kind of converged in the early '80s when people were really afraid of what was going on and were already wary of gay people. As the disease is going more national, you had more concern of how contagious it was and the idea for a while of whether you want to quarantine people. It got pretty intense.

From his position on the metro desk, Jeff did not risk openly pushing for coverage of gay subjects, lest unwanted attention be drawn to his own sexual orientation. Instead, he cannily operated through surrogates, especially straight reporters whom he perceived as being sensitive and educable. The clearest example of this indirect method of making change was a two-part series in 1983 on gay life amid the AIDS crisis. The second of the articles, which had a national focus, was written by Dudley Clendinen, a gay reporter who was so deeply closeted at the time that he had a wife and children. (He later divorced and came out.) For the opening piece, set in New York City, Jeff turned to one of the most gifted writers on metro, Michael Norman. As a Marine veteran of the Vietnam War and a suburban husband and father, Norman was as immune as possible from suspicions of favoritism or special pleading on behalf of gays.

Michael Norman

Millones came walking out to my desk one day. It must have been sometime in March or April '83 and he said, "You know, this AIDS thing is getting pretty big." (No shit, Peter.) "We want you to get medical background from Larry Altman and write a huge take-out on gay life in New York." I said, "Okay, fine, let me figure out where to start and do some reading on my own." I went right out of the office to the newsstands in Times Square and I picked up *The Advocate*, a couple of other gay papers, and I called Gay Men's Health Crisis.

When I got back in the office, I was walking up the hallway, and all of a sudden I see Jeff headed right for me. He got about three inches from my nose and said, "You know, of course, I'm gay." I did. He said, "Anything I can do to help. You're going to need help on this."

I went to some Y's that had discussion groups of gay men, and I touched base with some of Larry Kramer's commandos. And I would go back to Jeff from time to time. I don't know who initiated the conversation, Jeff or me, but at some point, I said, "This isn't working. I need to talk to gay men who aren't sitting in a circle in a meeting." So first Jeff gave me the names of four or five gay bars. I would go into them, sit on a stool, buy a guy a drink, and tell him what I was doing. And no one refused to talk to me, though a few wanted to remain anonymous.

I went back to Jeff and said, "The bar scene was good, but there's also all these clubs." And it was delicate, because the gay clubs were participatory. I said to Jeff, "Under no circumstances am I taking off my clothes for the story. You can describe the clubs to me."

But he did take me into three clubs. I remember one was very cavernous, and to get in, we had to take off our shirts. So I took off my shirt and I walked in and Jeff—the wonderful thing about Schmalz that only people close to him understood was his great sense of humor, his sharp wit—was getting the biggest kick out of this, his straight reporter on assignment with his shirt off. And he'd pull me by the elbow to meet this person or that person. He would walk me up to someone and say, "Hi, this is my good friend Michael, he's here for a visit, trying to figure out what he makes of this club." Everybody was pretty well-humored about it. And then he showed me around the club—in one corner, two men having oral sex, in another corner are guys who had on black leather jock straps, there was a lot of kissing and smooching. I was there to see what I was there to see.

Then we went to two other smaller clubs. It must have been 3:30 or 4 in the morning before I made it home. I don't know how much of that material got into the piece, but it had a big impact on me. I had no idea of gay nightlife. I remember thinking to myself, from a public-health standpoint, I didn't see any warnings about safe sex, all the things Larry Kramer was demanding. I saw none of that and remember thinking, *This is going to get a lot worse before it gets better.*

After I got all my material, the one editor I could talk to was Jeff. He gave me 99 percent of the guidance I got. None of the other editors wanted to talk about this story. I couldn't get straight answers out of anyone. Peter Millones was straitlaced. A couple of editors asked, "Has anyone put the moves on you yet?" Or they'd say, "How's the story going?" and sort of snicker. Their response, homophobically, was this sort of calculated indifference.

Jeff went over that story with me the way he went over every story I did. He would trace his right index finger across the computer screen, trace every sentence. "This paragraph here, we can move it there." Oddly enough, Millones's marching order—"We want to write about this as if you're writing about the Daughters of the American Revolution"—Jeff knew what he meant. Don't be an advocate. Be balanced and neutral. I was afraid of the story being prurient and titillating. I wanted it to be almost ethnographic. Just as I'd written about the oystermen of New Jersey. The same way as if the assignment was to write about Mennonites in Pennsylvania.

And Jeff brought that understanding to the story. He said he wanted it to be "a *New York Times* story." I was well aware the impact that this story would have. And part of Jeff's job was to shield me from any pressure. After the story ran, I remember Jeff coming up to me, and he smiled and gave me a pat on the back and said, "Good job." And that was enough for me. That was like getting the Medal of Honor.

June 16, 1983

HOMOSEXUALS CONFRONTING A TIME OF CHANGE

By MICHAEL NORMAN

In neighborhoods throughout the city and across a broad spectrum of New York life, the influence of homosexual men and women is being seen and felt more than ever before.

The yearly Gay Pride March, scheduled for June 26, is only one sign of the broadened awareness of homosexuality and the changes it has brought over the last decade and a half. The staffs of major political figures include representatives to the homosexual community. Homosexual churches and neighborhood groups have attracted hundreds of members. And this month a successful Broadway play about a drag queen's search for the meaning of family life won two Tony awards.

Still, there are quarters in which homosexuals encounter hostility, and many men and women continue to lead what they describe as double lives, "gay" at home and "straight" on the job. But shifts in public attitudes have prompted others to live openly.

In the last few months, however, the city's homosexual world has been shaken by the spread of a lethal disease, Acquired Immune Deficiency Syndrome, or AIDS. Its source is unknown, its cure not yet found. Half of the cases nationwide have appeared in New York, and 71 percent of them have afflicted homosexual men.

These numbers have done much more than just sour the atmosphere in the bars, baths and private clubs, where some men travel a circuit of drugs, alcohol and anonymous sex.

The epidemic has also created anxiety and caution in the homosexual community at large among those who lead a variety of life styles—individuals and couples whose lives are moored by work, home, family and friends.

The concern generated by the disease has led many people to suggest that it may change basic patterns of male homosexual life. It has already renewed a debate about homosexual morality.

Beyond all this, AIDS has focused attention on the difference in styles of life for homosexual men and women. It also has promoted a sense of unity in their community, tempering but not eliminating traditional differences caused by race, gender and social station...

...Nevertheless fear of disease has traveled through this large community as if it were a small town. The following account, offered by a 53-year-old man, a supplier of building materials, is typical of those reported in more than 50 interviews. Like more than half of those who agreed to talk, he asked not to be identified.

"My social life at this point is having dinner with good friends, playing backgammon and going to the theater," he said. "I had one very good friend who died of AIDS. Now I have another friend who is in the hospital with it. I know I'm clean, but I'm scared of everyone else."

Since the disease may be sexually transmitted, those who are attempting to study it have begun to look at social and sexual habits. Though there are prior studies, the homosexual community today is largely unmapped terrain. And thus most researchers and social observers say they can only report their impressions.

Alan R. Kristal, a doctoral candidate at the Columbia

University School of Public Health, has started a study to measure and characterize "gay sexual behavior." Like others in the homosexual community, he is quick to say that sexual styles among homosexuals are as diverse as they are among heterosexuals.

But he and others agree that the sexual awakening of the late 1960's and early 1970's had a particularly liberating effect on many homosexual men.

The reference point for this awakening, marked by the Gay Pride March, was June 28, 1969, the date of a police raid at the Stonewall Inn on Christopher Street, a bar for homosexual men. The raid led to a riot and the riot, many people say, gave birth to a social cause and sexual style.

"After Stonewall," Mr. Kristal said. "one thing that has been prevalent is that you socialize via sexual contact." The bars where homosexual men and women socialize range from chic disco palaces to neighborhood tap rooms. Some create an atmosphere for sexual contact. Other establishments have back rooms for private encounters. And there are the baths, with rented cubicles and large common rooms.

"There were always sleazy waterfront bars that were secret," said James M. Saslow, an editor of The Advocate, a homosexual newspaper distributed nationally. "When liberation came along, there was a proliferation of what we already had, more bars, bigger bars. What gay men wanted was easy anonymous sex with no attachments."

"I can remember the euphoria of the early days," said John J. Coveney, a self-employed real-estate holder in Chelsea. "We thought we were given license to be extreme."

Just four months after Norman's article appeared, Jeff Schmalz was reassigned off the metro desk. While he had been intending to move into reporting, his new posting in the paper's Connecticut bureau was the sort of low-prestige, low-visibility job usually given to a new hire as a kind of tryout. Privately, Jeff believed he had been sent to Connecticut in punishment for being gay—even though he continued to try to hide that fact from his superiors.

Change for gays and lesbians at The Times *came belatedly and abruptly when Abe Rosenthal was pushed into retirement as executive editor—he became an op-ed columnist—and Max Frankel took over the newsroom helm in October 1986. The next year, Arthur Sulzberger, Jr. was named assistant publisher, putting him into a position of significant influence over the newspaper. Going back to the early 1980s, when he was serving as an assignment editor on the metro desk and working closely with Jeff on a day-to-day basis, Sulzberger had been reaching out to gays and lesbians on the staff.*

Arthur Sulzberger, Jr.

I took him out to lunch and said, "So, Jeff, when are you going to tell me you're gay?" When you're that open and honest, he felt safe. We were friends. We had a relationship. On the desk, we trusted each other. We had worked through some management issues together.

In the outside world, it was becoming safer and safer and safer. One of the problems at *The Times* at that moment in our history was it was not seen as being safe. That's why you had to go out of the building to have that kind of a discussion. You wanted to help create a safe environment for your friends and colleagues. There were other colleagues who I did that to. It took a couple of months to get through those various lunches. They had to feel safe and you had to have an honest conversation.

David Dunlap

After Rich Meislin and I came out to one another in 1978, I began coming out selectively to people like Charlie Kaiser and others whom I knew to be gay so that the beginnings of a kind of network were set then. I came out to Steve Rattner, who'd been Scotty Reston's clerk the year before me and who was a close friend of Arthur. Steve indelicately but wonderfully passed the word about me onto him.

Arthur was then the metro assignment editor, and to his tremendous credit invited me out to lunch one day to say basically, "Steve Rattner's told me that you're gay. I think that's fine. That's great. Don't worry. I know people get worried around here. Don't worry." And back then, before we could even think of the possibility of gays having marriage and family, Arthur said in this wonderfully flippant way, "If it were up to me, the entire foreign staff would be gay, so that we wouldn't have to pay the expenses of moving families all around the world whenever we relocate correspondents." I knew, of course, that he was joking, but to have the heir presumptive tell you that as far as he was concerned everyone on the foreign staff, which was the highest pinnacle of correspondents, could be gay was a tremendous relief.

Richard Meislin

I remember the complete difference when Max took over. I became the head of graphics in 1988. I was dealing with the illness of a very close friend named Bob Barrios, who was a copy editor trainee on the foreign desk. He had been going through several terrible months and it was within days of the end for him. Max had lost his wife recently, so when they promoted me, Max brought me into his office for the sit-down and blessing of this newly created job as the head of graphics, which they then called editor of statistics news. Instead of talking about that, Max spent time talking about how hard it is to watch somebody that you love die. It was such an indication of the change that had happened that it was just mind-blowing.

Joseph Lelyveld

Shortly after I became managing editor in 1990, the gay and lesbian media workers had a Sunday afternoon forum at a meeting-house in Chelsea at which I and Paul Steiger of *The Wall Street Journal* both spoke and were asked questions. That was really interesting to me, because there were people in the audience from *The Times* who were coming out to me just by being there. Maybe they had come out, but there were a half-dozen people in the audience I hadn't thought of as gay who were there. All I remember about that event that was somebody asked, "When are you going to have gay wedding announcements in *The Times*?" At that moment I think I was thinking of Punch and said I thought we'd stop at having wedding announcements sooner than we'd print gay wedding announcements. But I knew Arthur Jr. would be for it.

Richard Meislin

For Gay Pride Day one year, we put up a sign in the newsroom: "We're having a party. We'd love to invite you but we don't know who you are." It was sort of the beginning of the gay and lesbian caucus at *The Times*. People started knowing who each other were. What was interesting was that the newsroom people were way overrepresented in this and the business-side people were sort of still more closeted than the news-side people were. It was clear that things were changing and clearly for the better.

Arthur was taking people out for lunch and asking them what it was like to be gay at *The New York Times*. When that question came from him, you dropped your fork because the message it was sending was, "I know, and it's okay."

One of concrete signs of institutional change came when Arthur Sulzberger, Jr. settled a new contract with the Newspaper Guild that allowed Times *journalists' domestic partners to receive healthcare coverage. In another indication of greater tolerance,* The Times *amended its style rules in 1987 to allow the use of "gay" rather than "homosexual" as an ordinary adjective.*

Allan Siegal

Max Frankel was very sympathetic to the concerns of the staff and very attuned to modern American speech in writing and felt that he was a new broom and he was going to have only one honeymoon and this was the time to make the changes. He got the change made to permit *gay*. These things all took a lot of internal wrangling and arguing. Max collected examples of other American publications that used gay for example and circulated them to senior editors and senior managers of the paper as examples of how far out of step we had become. One of the things he circulated was *TV Guide*. His point was that if you wanted to know what normal Americans were saying, you couldn't get more normal than *TV Guide*, and ultimately he prevailed.

It was very hard to avoid using a term like *gay* when all of society was using it. Increasingly, *homosexual* sounded freakish in writing. It didn't sound conversational. It didn't even sound normal. There were a lot of people crusading for us to make the change. Obviously the interest groups affected were crusading, but lots of our own staff were crusading. They didn't like having to write that way about people they were covering when they knew the preferences were different.

Arthur Sulzberger, Jr.

It just struck me that we don't have room for people to feel like they're the Other in our lives. That's true whether you're a woman or whether you're black or whether you're gay. We've got to embrace people and that's what our society is about. I've never felt other than that, honestly. I think it just came from being a part of the generation that grew up in the '60s and saw the Civil Rights movement, saw the anti-war movement, and participated in these things where people came together around ideas that allowed us all to grow.

The greater tolerance inside The Times *did little, however, to still the critics of its AIDS coverage. In 1987, the playwright-novelist-producer Larry Kramer led the formation of ACT UP, a group that practiced a militant, confrontational form of AIDS activism. Its approach was distilled in its mantra: "Silence=Death." Facing their own mortality, ACT UP members railed against politicians and scientists for not moving rapidly enough in a search for a cure, against the Catholic Church for its teachings on the sinfulness of homosexuality, and against the mainstream media for inadequately reporting on the AIDS crisis. The group's specific targets included Mayor Edward I. Koch, Cardinal John O'Connor, the Reagan and Bush administrations, and* The New York Times.

One of ACT UP's broadsides was an imitation newspaper that used The Times' standard fonts and was called The New York Crimes. In August 1989, ACT UP took its direct action to the home of the publisher, Arthur O. Sulzberger, Sr. On a Monday evening, activists drew the outlines of corpses on the sidewalk near Sulzberger's building and put up stickers with the slogan, "All The News That Kills." The next day, about 150 ACT UP members picketed outside the publisher's Upper East Side apartment and then marched to the Times office on West 43rd Street. With each location protected by about 200 police officers, the disproportionate show of force further incensed the marchers. Blocked from the Times' entrance, the ACT UP delegation issued a written demand to meet with Sulzberger and Frankel and offered its withering verdict of the newspaper's AIDS coverage:

AIDS CRISIS ESCALATES

WHILE NY *TIMES* SLEEPS

AIDS is the biggest medical news story of the twentieth century. But apparently *The New York Times* and Publisher Arthur "Punch" Sulzberger, whose family owns 70% of *The New York Times* Company, think differently. We gather here tonight to accuse Sulzberger and *the Times* of being accomplices in more than 55,000 American AIDS deaths, by choosing to minimize the importance of this disease and the people it strikes.

The Times is known as the "newspaper of record," whose coverage influences public opinion, lawmakers and journalists everywhere. When the world's leading newspaper runs incompetent AIDs coverage, it sends the clear message around the world that the epidemic is not a crucial story. This is not merely bad journalism—what amounts to an AIDS news blackout has already cost thousands their lives...

LET THE NEW YORK TIMES KNOW THAT ITS REPORTING OF THE AIDS EPIDEMIC IS INEFFECTIVE AND MORALLY REPREHENSIBLE.

While the controversy about The Times *continued and the death toll from AIDS mounted, Jeff Schmalz was released from his exile in the Connecticut bureau to become a reporter in, and then chief of,* The Times' *Albany bureau. There he led the coverage of Governor Mario Cuomo, a rising star in national politics and a tantalizingly undeclared, is-he-or-isn't-he candidate for the presidency in 1988, sometimes ridiculed as "Hamlet on the Hudson." Jeff's reporting earned him the friendship and admiration of colleagues like Elizabeth Kolbert and competitors like Adam Nagourney, the* Daily News' *Albany correspondent. It also regularly pricked Cuomo's famously thin skin.*

Elizabeth Kolbert

Jeff would come in late and the day would start in a very leisurely way. That was true of Albany, too. That was the rhythm of Albany;

people sort of wandered in. Then toward afternoon, as we were getting into the series of front-page meetings and things like that, things would really ramp up into this almost frenzy of excitement, because we in Albany always thought we had a front-page story. One thing I remember very distinctly is Jeff smoked unfiltered Camels. Smoke would start to emanate from his cave-like room. Such was Jeff's influence on me that I also tried to smoke unfiltered Camels, but I just really couldn't stomach it. Then we would get to a real crescendo right at deadline.

You had to file by eight p.m. Everything would get filed at the last second. We'd crash it in and then we would go out drinking. I also learned to drink from Jeff. I learned to drink martinis. I drank them extra dry like Jeff did. The whole Gestalt was very much Jeff. I will always think of it that way. I will always think of those afternoons and evenings and the rhythm that Jeff really established, part of which was the rhythm of journalism and part of which was the rhythm of Albany, but all of which was inflected by Jeff.

The Cuomo people would send someone over to *The Times* to get the early edition when it came out at eleven o'clock. Then I don't honestly know whether they woke the governor up, who was probably asleep by that point because he was a very early riser. Maybe they didn't, but maybe he got it then when he woke up at five in the morning. That's when I think he or one of his people would be on the phone to Jeff. Now that sort of colloquially became known as the "press war" in typical grandiose terms.

Adam Nagourney

Mario Cuomo was a really tough person to cover. I learned how to cover him in no small part from Jeff. I'll tell you what happened here. It was pretty early in my career and I had written a story and was a little bit on tender hooks in my job at *The Daily News*. I got a call at seven o'clock in the morning. It was Cuomo, who's complaining about whatever story I wrote and said, "You cut off my testicle." Just like that. He went into this long critique of my coverage. I was freaked out. I did not know what to do. I was up there and tentative *Daily News* bureau chief but I was sort of on trial up there. I never had been attacked like that before. I was really freaked out. I think that night I had dinner with Jeff and was debating whether or not to tell him about it, because we're also competitors. Eventually, I told him about it, and he looked at me and said, "Well, did you write it down?" I said, "No, I never thought about it." He said, "Everything is on the record. When he calls you like that, that's a story. That tells you what the governor of New York is like. You should keep a notebook by your bed and when he does stuff like that, you should write about it." So that's how I proceeded covering Mario Cuomo and every other politician I cover to this day. It was a great lesson.

Ultimately, Mario Cuomo did not run for president, and in 1988 Jeff was named Miami bureau chief, a position he held for the next two years. By the end of the 1980s, AIDS had killed nearly 40,000 people in the United States, the preponderance of them gay men.

To all outward appearances, Jeff remained healthy. His newsroom friends back in New York, however, could not help but worry.

Michael Specter

Jeff used to come down to my apartment on Friday nights and we would hang out for a while. Then we would go off to our separate places. I think Jeff's separate place was the piers and God knows what. I had always thought, "Gee, it's kind of weird that Jeff is healthy, because his practices are not the practices of a person who stays healthy at this time." I had worried about it and asked him and he said, "I'm HIV negative." At the time, it could have been true. I didn't say, "Show me your test results." I don't think he was lying to me, but it also seemed improbable. He was very sexually active in the way that you didn't want people to be at that time, that Larry Kramer didn't want people to be. A lot of gay men were still in the mindset of "Fuck you, this is my sexual freedom. You're not going to interfere with it."

Anna Quindlen

I thought of Jeff as a bathhouse kind of guy. That scared the hell out of me, to be honest, because that was an era where you were much more likely to read a story in the paper about some smart, high-achieving professional guy who had brought somebody home and then gotten his head bashed in.

I can remember sitting at the desk as the deputy metro editor with my coffee in front of me and Peter Millones would be sitting there and the other editors would be filing in—Jim Gleick, Tom Morgan. No Jeff, no Jeff, and I'd just think, "I'm terrified." I was terrified that he was going to pick up the wrong person. Of course, he did pick up the wrong person at some point, just not in the way that I was worried about.

PART TWO: CRACKED WIDE OPEN

The afternoon of December 21, 1990, was a comparatively quiet one on the National desk of The New York Times. *Nearly all of the stories vying for front-page display the next day involved foreign news: A civil defense drill in Baghdad, as Iraq anticipated an American invasion in response to Saddam Hussein's conquest of Kuwait. The tenuous place of liberal reformers in Mikhail Gorbachev's Russian government. Lech Walesa's impending inauguration as president of Poland.*

Of the eight articles bound for the front page, in fact, only one was being handled by Jeff Schmalz in his new role as deputy national editor—the governor of Ohio granting clemency to 25 women who had been imprisoned for killing or injuring men who had physically abused them. Also passing through Jeff's computer that day was an article by medical reporter Gina Kolata with particular interest for gay readers inside or outside The Times. *It conveyed the latest grim news about the epidemic that had already killed nearly 60,000 Americans.*

In a move that is widely viewed as boding ill for the approval of new AIDS drugs, a Federal administrator in charge of setting the guidelines on what drugs can be sold has asked to be transferred from her position.

A spokesman for the Food and Drug Administration said the administrator, Dr. Ellen C. Cooper, wants to leave her position because the stress has become too great . . .

Many federal administrators, researchers and advocates for people with AIDS said they were distressed that Dr. Cooper was leaving at what they view as a critical time. They said that two new drugs for AIDS will soon be reviewed for market approval and that the agency will soon decide whether to allow additional indicators that AIDS drugs are effective. Dr. Cooper, they said, has the sort of expertise that will be hard to replace.

Even so, this was the last Friday before Christmas, the start to a weekend of parties and shopping. In the Times *newsroom, as in just about every workplace, people were looking forward to leaving early to start the revelry. Then there was a sudden thud and a commotion.*

Richard Meislin

I was in the newsroom the day that Jeff collapsed and it was horrible. He basically had a seizure and fell to the floor. The newsroom just went into motion to get an ambulance on site. Nobody understood why it was, including Jeff, although I suspect that he suspected once he regained consciousness.

Max Frankel

I was at my office and Jeff happened to sit outside of it. I came back from lunch and heard he'd collapsed and they'd taken him into a little room right next to my office. So I went in, saw what had happened. The nurse chased me out and a few minutes later they were taking him to the hospital. And as they began to wheel him out of the city room, he came around and I took his hand and I spoke a few words to him. He said something about, "I think I'll be alright, I just fainted."

Michael Specter

Alessandra Stanley, who was then my wife, was in the newsroom when he had the seizure. She called me instantly and said, "They just took Jeff out on a stretcher. He had a seizure. What do you think's going on?" I said, "I'm not a doctor, but I think you'd have to put your money on HIV, because he's a healthy young gay man. That's what people have seizures about."

Wendy Schmalz Wilde

I found out the night of our office Christmas party at the literary agency. It was probably around 8 o'clock at night and I was still having one for the road with a friend of mine when the phone rang. It was someone at *The Times*, I don't remember who anymore, who said that Jeff had had a seizure in the newsroom and was rushed to St. Clare's Hospital and that I should probably get there as quickly as I could. I jumped in a cab and off I went.

Rich Meislin had gone with him. I had never met Rich before. He met me and told me that Jeff had a grand mal seizure and collapsed in the newsroom. That's all any of us knew. We weren't allowed to see him because they were running tests. Maybe an hour or hour and a half later, Jeff comes out looking slightly rumpled—but only slightly—and said, "What are you doing here? I am fine. Why did they call you?" I said, "I don't know. They called me. You came in an ambulance and I'm here. What do you want me to do? Are you all right?"

He said, "Let's go to Joe Allen's and have some dinner." I said, "Do you think that's a good idea?" He's like, "Absolutely. I'm fine. Let's just go to Joe Allen's and have some dinner."

I knew that he wasn't fine and I remember when the phone rang and they told me what happened I said to my friend at the office, "It's happened." He said, "What do you mean?" I said, "My brother has AIDS." I knew it. I just knew it. I had noticed probably for a few years that he often had rashes that he couldn't explain. He was always scratching his leg. He often had swollen glands, so when we were driving around, he'd loosen his shirt and say, "I don't feel well. I have a sore throat." I always thought, *He has AIDS and he's not telling me.* He was so private that I didn't say, "Have you been to a doctor? Have you checked this out? Have you done anything about this?" Even the night when he had the seizure, I don't think AIDS came up.

On January 25, 1991, Jeff attended his sister Wendy's wedding to her longtime boyfriend, Michael Wilde. The couple had deliberately moved up the date because of Jeff's condition.

Michael Wilde

We knew he was sick, but nothing had been diagnosed yet. His face was very, very red and he'd had a series of disturbing illnesses, so the writing was on the wall. It's one of the reasons for our hastiness in getting married: I realized it was then or never. I knew it in my bones and I wanted to go through this together with Wendy as her husband and Jeff's in-law.

I first encountered him on the steps of the Brooklyn [State] Supreme Courthouse, fifteen minutes before I became his brother-in-law. I was out of breath and nervous, hurrying up and down the staircase, searching for my sister, who had gone off for a smoke, when I happened upon Jeff, who was conducting a search party of his own. "Our side is here," is the quote.

Up to that point, I had seen only one picture of Jeff, an overexposed snapshot of a cigar and a blue sport shirt making its way out of frame with great haste, one hand waving. Since for three and a half years, I had only seen one picture, I was looking forward to meeting the blue shirt and the cigar with a mustache, but the rest was a mystery; I recognized him instantly. He was dapper and imposing, a trench coat draped over one arm. I reached up to shake his hand, on account of the staircase, and introduced myself.

I never knew the old Jeff, before the metamorphosis. I met him once, that day at the courthouse in Brooklyn, but it was only for a couple of hours—and even then he already knew. During a toast he made at our wedding, reading between the lines as brother and sister do, I heard words to our good health and future happiness; what she saw was an extremely flushed, preoccupied Jeff, revealing his deepest anxieties about his own health by wishing us the future he knew he wouldn't have. The next day brought us wine and roses; for Jeff, it brought multiple seizures.

The first of the seizures occurred in front of Jeff's mother at her home in Pennsylvania after Jeff had driven her and several other relatives back from his sister's wedding.

Wendy Schmalz Wilde

Now he obviously had to have tests done. He called me the day he got the diagnosis. We had dinner and he was completely unsentimental and said, "This is what we're going to do. You're probably going to have to take care of me," because that was my role in his life. "This is what I want for my funeral. Don't tell Mom, because she shouldn't know yet. We have to figure out what we're going to do." Very businesslike, over dinner and martinis. It was just like he was going away for vacation and I had to feed his fish.

In February 1991, he had a brain biopsy. That's when they discovered he had PML, which is a progressive brain infection. He was really given very little time to live, a few months. Again, he was all business. It was never "Poor me" or "Oh, my God, I'm dying" or "What am I going to do?" but just always, "This is what we're going to do and this is how we're going to handle it." He was always in charge.

During the seven months following his seizure, Jeff was hospitalized six times. He survived pneumonia as well as brain surgery. His T-cell count, a measure of the immune system's health, was two. The normal range is 500 to 1,500 (per cubic millimeter). In response, Jeff named his cells Frick and Frack. Finally, in the late spring of 1992, Jeff returned to the Times *newsroom.*

Max Frankel

One day he came in and told me, "I'm gay and I have AIDS and the doctors don't hold out too much hope." We thought he'd be dead within three, four months. "And I don't know what I want to do." And the rest was almost mechanical after that first human encounter with reality. And it was a heroic act, because he wasn't just telling me he was ill, he was telling me about his whole life and what he thought it meant, and how he was visibly changing his own approach to himself and to others. And all of that was encapsulated into this 60-second conversation.

Soma Golden Behr

Until he got sick, Jeff was zero out. That was one of the great sadnesses about it, because everyone knew Jeff was gay. It was no secret in the newsroom that Jeff was gay. It's also no secret that there'd been people in the newsroom that were not so nice to people who were gay, former big bosses and all that. But this was a different era. This was Max Frankel and Arthur Sulzberger, Jr. trying to be the liberal guys, and this is me. I would tell Jeff so many personal stories in order to try to get him to open up. We would talk about things that had happened in my life; I just tried to show him, "I'll show you a card if you show me one." He never did.

You would have thought that he would have felt like he could open up. I don't know how he rationalized that in his head. We were really in sync on so many things, but he didn't trust me enough. What did he think? What did he think that I would ever possibly do to hurt him except to try to understand him better?

The first conversation I had with Jeff after he knew he was sick and I knew he was sick was when he came to see me in the office. We sat down. He sat across from me and said, "I have to tell you that I have AIDS and am HIV-positive." And I said, "I'm really sorry. I'm devastated." I'll always remember he said with his hands, "Well, you know, I'm gay." This was the first time he had ever said to me that he's gay. He'd never acknowledged it and he did it with a flourish. I said, "Yeah, I know, Jeff." To me, it was like, oh, my God, how did he live in such a shadow of who he was? How did he manage that? How does he say now to me, "You know I'm gay?" Well, yeah, everybody knew you were gay. Couldn't you have maybe let us in your window, let us know you better, let us help you?

I don't think it was his ambition, as some people said. I don't think that's what it was. He was gay and everyone knew it and there was nothing going to put that back out of his life. That was who he was. If he'd owned it I don't think he would have been less competitive. It was not Abe Rosenthal's era. It was on the way to what we have now, which is that people don't even notice who's gay. It's so sad. We're all victims of our history.

Wendy Schmalz Wilde

After Jeff got the diagnosis for the brain infection, I told my mom he had AIDS. That's the way she found out he was gay. She'd been in complete denial. I think as a single mother she was very worried that there was no father figure and that this was her fault and there should have been a man in his life and there wasn't. So she was heartbroken. She was just devastated. He was the light of her life. One night in October of 1991, about 10 months after his first seizure, I finally said to her, "He's not going to get better. He's going to die." She dropped dead that night. She hadn't been sick at all. I think she had a heart attack or a stroke. I think she truly died of a broken heart.

Even as he presented an indomitable front in the newsroom, Jeff privately descended into depression, fearing he would be unable to write again. But with the 1992 presidential primaries underway, he accepted the assignment to follow the campaign trail. While initial articles primarily concerned the three emerging candidates—

President Bush, Bill Clinton, and Ross Perot—Jeff also devoted a lengthy article in October 1992 to the growing political clout of the gay community. He was surprised and struck by how much positive feedback he received from readers, especially those who were gay.

Joseph Lelyveld

Assigning him to the 1992 campaign was an easy shot. He had done at least one important piece for the magazine in that period. [A profile of Mario Cuomo, who was expected to be a candidate.] He was an accomplished political reporter with all that Albany experience behind him. That way, you didn't have to look around for an empty slot to put him in. He was of a stature that you didn't really want to just give him a narrow slot or beat.

Adam Moss

I had an unusual way of meeting Jeff. I came into the paper as a consultant and worked for Joe Lelyveld, but I didn't have a specific portfolio. No one knew what to do with me. I was a kind of weird outlier at *The Times*. They physically situated me in a kind of alcove of the newsroom. There were three desks at the alcove of the newsroom. I was there all by myself for a while and then one day this desk next to me was about to be filled by Jeff.

Jeff hadn't been regularly back at *The Times* since he had collapsed in the newsroom. Before then, he'd been very much an establishment figure of *The Times*. He came back a very different person. He came back not only an ill person but also grappling with, and somewhat liberated by, his new outness in a newsroom that did not have many out gay people. I was a younger out gay person from a slightly different generation, and so Jeff and I would talk about gay stuff all the time. I had been out for a long time, relatively comfortable being out. This was all brand new for Jeff. He was like a little boy in some ways, even though it came with, in his case, this horrible awareness that the other side of it was this illness that he had. What was also very weird was that the third desk—it was three desks in a row—was filled by an older gay man named Hal Gal [a longtime editor in the Style and Home sections]. Nobody did this on purpose, but you had three generations of gay men next to each other in this kind of separate alcove in the newsroom. It was basically like a gay knitting circle and we would talk about these things.

Jeff did not rail in bitter terms to me about *The Times*' coverage of gay issues. It was more because he was implicated in that. He was a deputy editor of the National desk when he collapsed. He was in a position to do all sorts of things on AIDS coverage and gay coverage and he didn't, for the most part. He had a reflective tone about all of that and trying to make sense of it. He was being kind of awakened as an activist and trying to also reconcile an activist animus or personality with the reporter's personality and the editor's personality and the establishment personality that he had at *The New York Times* for years and years before that.

As Jeff used his campaign coverage to begin reporting on gay issues, he interviewed Larry Kramer of ACT UP. In that encounter, as in many interviews to come with other sources who had HIV or AIDS, Jeff found himself dropping the mask of the detached reporter.

Schmalz: I'm a little confused actually. The more I report this piece, the more confusing it becomes.

Kramer: Indeed.

Schmalz: Because it just seems to go off in 50 different directions at once. You have, on the one hand, this is a great moment really for gay people and politically we're sort of coming-of-age here. We're not shut out anymore. We are a constituency that's tolerated, that is sought out. Maybe I'm wrong, but I think that should be a time of getting it together. On the other hand, it seems to be falling apart in a lot of different ways. It's falling apart in ACT UP. I think the coalition in terms of the lesbian/gay relations is beginning to crack a little. People are torn at AIDS, which is killing us and yet in another way empowering us. It just seems to me so confusing I can't quite . . .

Kramer: I think that's exactly right. You put it in a nutshell. That is the problem. Now to ask how well put together it was in the first place instead of falling apart. It was never put together well, nor could it have been. We're all brand new at all of this. Most of us didn't want to get involved in it.

Just about everybody working in AIDS is not interested and didn't get interested in it because they were in politics, but just because they wanted to save their lives.

Toward end of the interview, with Jeff's topical questions answered, the tone veered even deeper into the personal, with two very ill men comparing medical notes.

Kramer: Are you on top of all the latest things to take?

Schmalz: I'm right now strictly on AZT after much—[my doctor] is against doing any combination therapy right now, because I've been doing so incredibly well. A year and a half ago, I had brain surgery. I have PML, which usually you die after four months. It's been quite amazing that I'm walking around. His feeling is that since I'm doing so well with AZT, let's keep pushing it and see how long we can go on it. Some people can go for some time on it, while other people usually get the 18 months. We're hoping I can go a little longer on it. If I can't, then we'll have to go to DDI [didanosine, an anti-retroviral drug], but DDI is not as effective on brain—it doesn't cross the blood-brain barrier very well . . . We'll see. Everything is a crapshoot, as you know.

During the late summer of 1992, Jeff increasingly shifted into covering AIDS full-time. He did so partly at his own behest and partly as The Times' *response to critics of its AIDS coverage, led by ACT UP. While* The Times *had been covering the medical side of the AIDS crisis since 1981, Jeff showed the human face of the epidemic, specializing in personal profiles that were at once compassionate and unflinching. In the process, he also depicted AIDS's spread from its initial epicenter among gay men and intravenous drug users into a wide spectrum of society.*

Anna Quindlen

I went to see him at his apartment. He was extremely thin. I think the T-cell count was down into single digits. We acted like everything was fine. I mean, no, we didn't. We acted like it was a story. What was he going to cover next? What was the story that hadn't been done yet? Was there a magazine piece in it? Was there a first-person piece in it? We talked about it like it was a story. We were talking about the beat, the beat, which encompassed his poor frail body.

Wendy Schmalz Wilde

I think he at first didn't want to be part of the story, and I think there's a certain amount of denial that goes with that. "This can't be happening to me. I'm not one of them." Then he realized that he had a bit of a moral obligation, because he had the bully pulpit and needed to go out and start beating the drum a little bit. That's what motivated him. He decided in the end that he needed to be more politically active with respect to AIDS, that he couldn't live with himself and sit back and not voice his own feelings and what he felt people should be doing. I think he struggled with that quite a bit.

Max Frankel

When he first came back to the office after looking after himself medically and encountering many other people who had AIDS and all their struggles, he consciously talked about how he wanted to report in the field of AIDS because of what he had learned. A whole new world had opened up that he never knew existed, and he thought it was interesting, dramatic, and important, and he wanted to write about it. And we briefly said, write about it or begin to be its champion and advocate, and he pursued that objective. He's pushed our boundaries of writing and reporting, but he has held to our values, and I think he has been fully honest with the reader, which is the ultimate test.

It sounds difficult and it is difficult to carry off, when you come up against emotional situations and you've covering other people who have AIDS and you're bringing them out of themselves and you want to interact with them as a human being, but it happens to all us. We're soldiers and we write about war, we're liberals and we write about liberals, we're women or we have an abortion and we write about abortion. We vote and we write about politics. We live two lives and have a professional ethic. It's not hard to develop that professional ethic if you believe in what you're doing and that there is a higher good in containing yourself and your own emotions. Every once in awhile you snap, but that's your professional ethic, and Jeff was a living example of it.

Eric Marcus

I think that editors and the public were suspicious of gay people in general reporting on gay issues, because how could we possibly be objective about this issue. It was still a time when there was a moral aspect to it in a way that we no longer talk about, at least in the mainstream. Whenever gay stories were reported, they were reported with "balance," and people would be called in, the most radically insane anti-gay people from groups like the Family Research Council. I often felt it was the equivalent of having a Nazi comment on the rights of Jewish people. I'm Jewish and feel I can say that.

In the late 1980s and early '90s, my book *The Male Couple's Guide* was first published. It was a simple guide for couples about their relationships, how to arrange insurance, who does the dishes, and how to divide responsibilities. I was terrified going out on the media tour. What I had to deal with was some shocking prejudice out in the world. On this show, *CNN News Night Update*, a guy called in who said, "Yeah, you gay people have rights. You have the right to be chained to my truck and dragged down the highway and to serve as target practice in my backyard." That was the world in which Jeff Schmalz operated. That's why his voice was so important and why his position at *The New York Times* leading the way for the rest of the country made such a difference, even though he had such a tiny window of time in which to do it.

Joseph Lelyveld

If you went to Times Square waiting for a red light, you'd see a little sticker on the lamppost saying, "Stop Gina Kolata" [*Times* medical reporter] or something to that effect. AIDS wasn't controversial in the sense that there were people in favor of AIDS and people against AIDS. It wasn't a conflict in that way. But we had the constant nuisance of Larry's group [ACT UP] campaigning against us. I got a certain amount of it, because my wife was running a daycare center in the Bronx for children with AIDS. Larry would in his polemics sometimes say, "The managing editor should know better than to print these articles, because his wife is doing noble work on the front lines." I even took him to lunch and said, "Do me a favor and just leave Carolyn out of it. You can attack me as much as you want, but she's doing her work. I'm doing my work. She's got nothing to do with what goes on here." Of course, he didn't.

I used to argue to Larry that he was the biggest believer in *The New York Times*, that he thought that the course of the disease, like everything else in America, was governed by what *The New York Times* did. If only. But putting Jeff on the beat was convenient. I don't think anybody said what I just said, "Let's do this. It's a good way to answer Larry Kramer." I don't think it was at that level. We had to decide to do something with Jeff. He was writing wonderfully and you wanted to keep him writing as long as he could for his own sake and the paper's. It was an exciting idea, as well as a difficult one, when you considered that on the basis of what anybody knew at the moment, it had a time limit on it or a near horizon.

Anna Quindlen

AIDS kicked in the closet door. There were people who might have stayed closeted their whole lives long who, when they got sick, when they had the marks on their face and on their arms, couldn't be closeted any more. Jeff wasn't closeted, but he wasn't as out as he became after his illness and when he wrote about it for *The Times*.

I think, in an odd kind of way, becoming ill liberated him to be who he was and even more than who he had been. It made him a better person. He'd be the first person to say that that it made him more human. Part of that was the understanding of suffering, but part of it I think was the openness. The closet made people hard, strange, and isolated in a way that isn't good for human beings.

It wasn't that Jeff's style changed. It was that Jeff's character changed. He became a different person when he became ill. He was incredibly skilled and I was enormously attached to him. But he could be really arrogant and judgmental when I first met him when he was younger. There was a sense that he was judging you harshly, because you'd messed up, because he could do it better, because he was more capable than you were. Which was almost always true, but it's not attractive. I hate to say it, because the trope of the person ennobled, opened up, humanized by terrible illness is such a cliché. In his case, it was completely true. He became a better writer because he became a better human.

Michael Specter

A lot of people wouldn't have associated the words empathy and compassion with Jeff before HIV became part of life, because he was a very directed, focused, driven, analytical editor. He was very systematic and precise and focused. A lot of people interpreted that as cold. Obviously, that isn't my view, and I don't think he was a cold person. But I don't think compassion was the word that leapt to mind for a generation of people who had to deal with him before HIV.

Wendy Schmalz Wilde

I think AIDS freed him in a lot of ways to be his true self. For a long time, he was very egocentric essentially. His ambition was his main force in life. When he became ill, he mellowed quite a bit. He was more willing to help other people and realized there was more in the world than climbing to the top of *The New York Times*.

Mary Fisher

I was diagnosed in 1991 with HIV. I went public in January of 1992. It was an amazing coming-out in the Detroit newspapers. Frank Bruni, who's now with *The New York Times*, wrote that article. I didn't know what happens now after that whole coming-out and making that decision of going public. A friend of mine in Washington said, "I think maybe we get you to the platform hearings." This was a big deal for me, because my father was so involved in the Republican Party. He was a finance chairman for Bush 41 at the time. For me to speak at the platform hearings, I really needed for him to give his blessing, because I needed to in many respects use him and say, this is my history. I can always say I worked for a Republican president, Ford, but I needed to use my father. Our family is just a very quiet family. We're not really an out-front family so this was brand new for us. I had a little bit of resistance from some family members but my father totally understood and agreed, which was remarkable and amazing.

The lead-up to the convention was that I had spoken at the platform hearings. Once they said that Elizabeth Glaser and Bob Hattoy were going to speak about AIDS at the Democratic convention, I thought it would be so great if we could get this done. The president himself wanted me to speak, but it was not an easy thing. It was, "You're kidding. You must be the only Republican with AIDS. Why do you want to speak at the Republican convention?" It was amazing to me that this is what people were thinking. That kind of buildup was getting me into a situation where they wanted a speech.

When *The New York Times* called, the buildup was that they gave me this spot on the Women's Night, which was a Wednesday. Once we had it, then the media started coming. Jeffrey was really the one to say, "I really want to do this story because it's not typical." He did want to know what I was going to say, but I couldn't tell him. It came with other stories that were happening, but it was his story in my mind that was the most important story that I did before the convention.

I was fearful of even having this interview because of who he was. I believed that he would be a tough interviewer, and the interview was tough for me. I knew I was walking a fine line. Before the convention, it seemed like I didn't have a whole lot of friends. The gay community was sort of afraid of me or what I was going to say in that setting. I felt alone and very isolated. I wasn't trained to do this. I was always the behind-the-scenes person. I was always the producer. I was never the talent. So for me it was difficult to try to get my message across.

To me, Jeff was being very tender in his gestures and quiet moments. I knew that the words he was using were tough. I don't know if that makes any sense. I remember his voice. I remember his voice being so strong but gentle. It isn't maybe anything that he said or did, but that strength that comes from knowing that you're doing what you love to do and also doing what you're passionate about and what you care about. I just remember knowing it was tough, but feeling that his energy was remarkable.

August 16, 1992

AIDS TEST

By JEFFREY SCHMALZ

AIDS is not a Republican disease.

To be sure, plenty of Republicans have died of AIDS, and plenty more are sick. But the party has never been comfortable talking about the disease. The epidemic was more than five years old before President Ronald Reagan uttered the "A" word publicly. The wrath of God, the right wing said. All those homosexuals and blacks and drug abusers.

Enter, now, Mary Fisher: very rich, very Republican and very much infected with the virus that causes AIDS. Just as Bob Hattoy stood before the Democratic National Convention last month and announced on nationwide television, "I am a gay man with AIDS," so will she stand before the Republican National Convention this week and announce that she is a Republican woman—one of their own—who is infected.

"It's something I feel I have to do," said Ms. Fisher, who is 44 years old. "It's my mission, my contribution to the fight against AIDS." She sat in her two-story living room here, where floor-to-ceiling windows look out onto a pond in a guarded, gated enclave of multimillion-dollar houses. She laughed at all the fuss about her being a speaker, at headlines like "Heiress Battles AIDS." Then she added: "This is hard. It's hard. It hasn't been easy for me."

Indeed, it has not. Ms. Fisher, who so far has not had any AIDS-related illnesses, is caught between the worlds of Republican politics and AIDS activism, both of them at times uneasy about her.

Party officials were more or less forced into letting her speak. Some felt they had to counter the poignant speeches before the Democratic Convention by Mr. Hattoy and, especially, Elizabeth Glaser, whose account of her family's battle with AIDS—the death of her 7-year-old daughter, the infection of her son and herself—moved delegates to tears. And then there was the clout of Ms. Fisher's father, Max Fisher, a Detroit real-estate investor who is a top contributor and fund-raiser for the Republican Party.

But even after giving her approval for the speech, the party is keeping an eye on her. Even as she chatted in her living room, a draft of her address was being faxed back and forth between her and the convention site in Houston for review, changes and counterchanges.

Wary, too, are advocates for people with AIDS. They wonder how critical she will be of the Bush Administration. And a few say she is allowing herself to be used as the AIDS poster girl by a party that they believe has done little to fight the disease or provide moral leadership.

In a sober, hourlong conversation about life and death, it was only when that criticism of her was raised that her eyes filled with tears . . .

. . . Like many people who are infected with the AIDS virus, she has found that it has given her a renewed look on life, a thrill at merely being alive.

"At first you think you're going to die the next day," she said of the moment in July 1991 when she found out she had the AIDS virus. "I thought I had bought the farm." Her husband, an artist from whom she was already divorced, had called a week before to say that he had tested positive and that she should be checked.

"I don't think of myself as being religious," she said. "But this has been a spiritual experience. I have come to believe that there's a purpose in life. It feels right. I've been able to bring together the experiences of my life, my politics, my Washington days."

If anything, the disease seems to have helped her find herself. Where before, her life was an unfocused blur of art and children, she now has a mission. She is coming into her own as a genuine force in AIDS circles, regarded as bright and committed, not as some dilettante who will move on to the next cause du jour . . .

. . . Always, her conversation comes back to the children, Max and Zachary. She has told them little about her infection, mostly because they are too young. "What anger there is, I work out because of the children," she said. "It's not good for them to be around that."

With that, she seemed to end the chat. But a few minutes later, at the door, she rushed up. "I want a big hug," she said. Then she threw open her arms, squeezing a reporter tight and whispered, "Stay well."

Eric Marcus

Jeff could do interviews of people who had AIDS in a way that other reporters who were not HIV-positive could not. There was a natural connection between Jeff and his subjects. It was natural for Mary Fisher to open up to Jeff in a way that she might not to another reporter, because she and Jeff were looking at the clock ticking. They knew that the likelihood was that they were going to be dead sooner rather than later. That was true for all the people that Jeff interviewed during those years. We forget how desperate the time was, how many people were dying then and how short the life expectancy was.

So for all the people Jeff interviewed who were HIV-positive, they were all facing their mortality in a way that I can't even begin to imagine. They trusted him with their stories in a way that they would not have trusted a straight male or female reporter. He had a unique position in writing about that. At *The Times*, he had this unique position, as well, in that he was dying. Everyone knew he was. I'm guessing that he was granted latitude that he wouldn't have been otherwise and because of his place in *The Times* and who he was. He shifted the profession in a way at *The Times* and other newspapers and other news outlets where reporters could write more personally. It was so effective. I imagine editors had to recognize that this was not only the right thing to do but a good thing.

Soma Golden Behr

A lot of people were still closed off to AIDS. "It's not in my life. I don't have to worry. That's some other bunch of gay crazy guys in New York." Jeff took that on when he wrote in a poignant way and said, "You'd better read this. This is about all of us." He didn't exclude people. He wasn't just writing to some small group of AIDS activists. He was writing to the heart of what has turned out to be every family in this country, which has turned out to be all these bigots who hid behind the façade and didn't let their kids be what they were and didn't recognize Cousin Timmy is gay. Jeff helped open that door. People nowadays are surprised how fast this country's turned around on gay rights. A big bunch of that came from Jeff's writing I think and really touched the hearts.

In the spring of 1993, Jeff interviewed Thomas Stoddard, a lawyer and longtime gay activist in the Lambda Legal Defense and Education Fund. They spoke in the wake of a march for gay rights and AIDS activism in Washington, and the ostensible subject of the conversation was the battle against the Clinton Administration's "Don't Ask, Don't Tell" policy on gays in the military. Inevitably, though, the subject turned to mortality.

Schmalz: What happens after you get on the military campaign?

Stoddard: I don't know. This almost for me makes me more existential. I don't plan my life. It would be foolish to plan my life. I don't know how long my life is going to go on. I don't know what it will hold in store. I don't know what my stamina will be. I feel my way through the rest of my life. This might sound crazy, but I feel optimistic and hopeful, because I've been able to survive with a diagnosis of full-blown AIDS for almost four years, which defies the statistics. I know that my sense of place in the world gives me some incentive to move on. I don't know what I'm going to be doing six months from now. I'm trying to stop myself from even thinking about it.

Schmalz: It just stalks you . . .

Stoddard: I think I will not survive.

Schmalz: So this keeps you going. It keeps you alive.

Stoddard: It's part of my regimen. It's part of my medication.

Schmalz: There's some denial on that, isn't there?

Stoddard: I don't think it's denial. I don't know what my life has in store for me. I never thought I'd have this illness. In many ways, I'm privileged. I want to evaluate my entire existence every day, figure out what I should be doing and move forward. This illness makes me concentrate my being on day-to-day business and to reevaluate and reconceive my existence every moment. It's an exhausting endeavor. One of the reasons why I find it so hard—but it also is thrilling—is because it permits me to deal with the big issues of human existence every moment. I don't have the luxury to float along in my life. If I floated along in my life, I'd be dead now.

Schmalz: You have a different approach to this. I go on the assumption that this is going to kill me and I'm not going to be around in a couple of years.

David Dunlap

Jeff had worked for months to get to speak with Clinton. I think the way it finally played out was Clinton was being shuttled in the presidential limousine from one spot to another. The idea was, "Schmalz, you can ride with him from point A to point B. That's the time you have with him." That's how it had to be, so I guess the president was already in the car and Jeff clambers into the presidential limousine. It is said that he said to Clinton, "How does it feel to be in the backseat of a car with a known homosexual?"

Much of their talk was policy—Clinton opposing discrimination but not wanting to deal with issues like marriage that connote acceptance of the "homosexual lifestyle"—but it also took a more personal turn.

Clinton: I just think in the last two years knowing people who had AIDS, having a friend die of AIDS, made a big difference. It just sort of made me more comfortable in dealing with it.

Schmalz: Who was the friend who died?

Clinton: A friend of mine in Little Rock died from AIDS a few years ago. I'd rather not name it.

Schmalz: Is a nice boy from Little Rock comfortable talking about all these issues?

Clinton: Yeah, I think my mother's okay about it. I came from a family, when I was in Hot Springs growing up as a kid, there were at least two people in my community that everybody knew were gay. They did their jobs, had friends. Now and then, there were snickers behind their backs, but there was no overt persecution. Nobody ever stopped to have them removed from their practice of their professions. I don't know whether they would have had they said it. This is more about saying than doing. This whole thing is.

Schmalz: And all about AIDS.

Clinton: I think a lot of it is.

Schmalz: When you see your friends dying and say, "The hell with it."

Soon after Clinton won the election, Jeff turned his reportorial attention to a different kind of public figure—the basketball star Magic Johnson. The leader of championship teams with Michigan State in the NCAA and the Los Angeles Lakers in the NBA, Johnson had made international news on November 7, 1991, by announcing he was infected with HIV, apparently as a result of his active extramarital sex life as a heterosexual. Despite the infection, he won a gold medal in the 1992 Olympics as part of the U.S.A.'s basketball "Dream Team." As he spoke with Jeff, Johnson had just published his autobiography. The interview ended this way:

Schmalz: Let me ask quickly before we let you go. Do you like the name Magic? You've come to like it. You talk in the book about how you're not sure.

Johnson: I liked the name Magic when I was playing. It was great. Now I'm Earvin. I want people to know me as Earvin.

Schmalz: Okay, let's start that in The New York Times. We'll make sure you're Earvin. What was the date, Magic, you found out you were HIV-positive?

Johnson: It was the 25th?

Schmalz: I have it here. I was just curious if you had it emblazed in your memory or not.

Johnson: You know, I've got so many dates I can't remember, but I think it was the 25th.

Schmalz: What do you think: let's say it's 50 years from now, Magic, and you're about to kick the bucket. What would you like the obituary to say? Magic Johnson what?

Johnson: Magic Johnson who enjoyed life to its fullest every day. Magic Johnson who cared and tried to help people. He got that from his mom.

Schmalz: She'll be pleased.

Johnson: Magic Johnson who left and didn't want anybody

to feel sorry for him or sorry that he passed. A young man who enjoyed his life, who's been on both sides of the fence; who's been poor and been successful. Who wanted young people to realize to do hard work. They think it's just a cliché or a word thrown out there all the time, but I know it's true. Do hard work and you can become what you want to.

Schmalz: It's interesting you didn't say, "Magic Johnson, one of the great or perhaps the greatest basketball star of all times."

Johnson: No. I always wanted to be more than a basketball player. I think I'm becoming that. I don't want people just to remember me as that. There was a lot more to me I hope than just that.

Schmalz: It's sort of ironic that it took HIV to do that for you, isn't it?

Johnson: Yeah. I was dreaming that all my life. You're right. It took HIV to bring that.

Schmalz: To give you a whole new dimension and a whole new persona. The kind that you were seeking for.

Johnson: It's really weird.

Schmalz: There are these pluses. Every negative has a bit of a plus.

That exchange gave form and focus to the resulting article.

November 19, 1992

ON THE BOOK-SIGNING CIRCUIT WITH MAGIC JOHNSON; CALL HIM EARVIN: 'I CAN'T BE MAGIC'

BY JEFFREY SCHMALZ

If ever there was a man of contradictions, it is Magic Johnson.

He is a 6-foot-9-inch powerhouse of arms and legs charging the court. Yet he can seem more like a teddy bear—huggable, with a boyish smile and a soft voice that says everything is all right.

He is a champion for those, like himself, infected with H.I.V., which causes AIDS. Yet this month he pulled out of basketball for a second time, giving in to the very prejudices he is committed to fighting. He waxes religious, sweet as a sermon on a Sunday morning. Yet he offers no apologies for his sexual escapades—and they were many.

If it is confusing to watch Magic, it is confusing to be Magic. He, more than anyone else, seems to be trying to figure out who he is these days, this superstar of sports with a disease that sports wants nothing to do with.

"I'm not Magic Johnson anymore," he said in a long, wrenching conversation the other day. "I'm Earvin Johnson now."

Such duality can be used as an excuse for inappropriate behavior, and that may be what Magic is up to. Yet, with his identity as a basketball star stripped away, he's in a never-

never land between Magic Johnson, the star, and Earvin Johnson, the guy next door, infected with H.I.V. At times, he even seems like a third person, a boy hanging out on the neighborhood courts, dreaming of one day being a great basketball star, dreaming of being Magic Johnson.

"I'd like to be Magic Johnson," he said. "But I can't."

Even in this sensitive, admiring portrait, Jeff inserted an astringent note. Never much of a sports fan himself, he still felt almost personally disillusioned by Magic Johnson's decision to retire from the NBA in 1993 in the face of opposition from fellow players who feared somehow being infected by him.

. . . if Magic feels betrayed by fellow players, so, too, do many fellow H.I.V. sufferers feel betrayed by him. They argue that by leaving competition, he has given legitimacy to what they view as irrational fears.

Magic seemed hurt when that point was pressed in the interview. He took on the look of a favored son crushed that his father is disappointed in him.

"People with the virus should know that that's been my life, playing basketball," he said. "I wanted to do it for them—for people with H.I.V.—more than anything else, more than for myself. I knew how important it was to them. But if I stayed and didn't do well because I wasn't having fun, people would say it was because of H.I.V. So the question was: Do I help the cause more by going or staying? I want to be that person who people with H.I.V. can still look to and say, 'You know what? He's carrying on.'"

In profiles like those of Fisher, Stoddard, and Johnson, Jeff infused an intimate tone into the third-person convention of a newspaper feature story. Having stretched the form, he then stepped entirely outside it, composing a first-person essay, a daring rarity in the news columns of The New York Times.

Michael Specter

When he wrote at the end about himself, he made me go over every word. He was so anxious about putting himself as a human being out there. He didn't have any anxiety about people knowing or writing on any number of subjects, but I think it was really hard for him to be a first-person writer. It's kind of sweet. He needed what we all need, but you didn't think Jeff needed, which was someone to say, "Yeah, this is a good story, this is worth doing"—particularly when he put himself into it.

December 20, 1992

COVERING AIDS AND LIVING IT: A REPORTER'S TESTIMONY
By JEFFREY SCHMALZ

TWO years ago tomorrow, I collapsed at my desk in the newsroom of The New York Times, writhed on the floor in a seizure and entered the world of AIDS.

I had been, as far as I knew, absolutely healthy, and it took the doctors a few weeks to reach their diagnosis: full-blown AIDS, with a brain infection often fatal within four months.

That I have lived these two years is a miracle. How long my luck will hold, no one knows. But for now, I am back working, a reporter with AIDS who covers AIDS.

I've thought a lot about my dual identity since the death last Sunday of Ricky Ray. I wrote about him and his family in 1988, about their new life in Sarasota, Fla. It was a year after their home was destroyed by arson in Arcadia, Fla., a town where many people hated Ricky and his two younger brothers because they were infected with H.I.V., a town where pickup trucks bore the bumper sticker "This vehicle protected by a pit bull with AIDS."

I recall my late-summer evening with the Rays vividly: Three barefoot boys in jeans and T-shirts, scrambling on the floor with their hamster. A sooty Garfield the Cat, himself a survivor of the fire, looking down from the china cabinet. "I'm only human," Garfield said when his string was pulled, and the Ray boys would turn giggly.

How proud I was of myself. How noble of me to write about these people nobody wanted to touch. How smug I was that I, a gay man, had escaped AIDS. (I know now that I was already infected. But I had not been tested; I felt great.) And how ambivalent I was about the Rays, these people who had parlayed personal tragedy into celebrity—they seemed just a little too available for interviews—and who talked so glibly of death.

Now, four years later, at the age of 39, it is I who talk matter-of-factly of life and death and who have used my affliction to advantage, to obtain interviews and force intimacy. Does that make me feel guilty? You bet. But to have AIDS is to live with guilt and shame.

So many tensions are at work on those of us with AIDS that it's hard to chronicle them. My mother, seemingly healthy, died last year at 73, a few months after my sister told her of my AIDS. A coronary? A stroke? Who knows? In my mind, it will always be a broken heart.

I make sure everyone with AIDS whom I interview knows that I have it, too. To be sure, that is an interview ploy; I'm hoping the camaraderie will open them up. But there is more to it than that: I want them to take a good look at me, to see that someone with full-blown AIDS can carry on for a while, can even function as a reporter. Much of the time, it works. Their faces light up. There is hope.

But sometimes it fails, and I am the one changed by our chat, overcome by guilt that I have lived these two years when so many of my friends and hospital roommates and people I've interviewed have died. At times, I think my fellow AIDS sufferers are laughing at me, looking up from their beds with eyes that say, "You'll be here soon enough."

Endlessly, I fret about my interviews. I know the buttons to push with people with AIDS and I push them well. Do I cross the line, pressing too hard for the sake of a good quote?

"I wish it wasn't true," Bob Hattoy said of having AIDS just before he addressed the Democratic National Convention. "But it isn't overwhelming me. Really. I don't know why."

I knew from my own experience the nightmares of waking up in a coffin, of wondering whether every cold was the big one that would do me in. I challenged him for not being honest, and he broke down. I wanted to hold him. I wanted to apologize. Then he hit me as hard as I had hit him.

"I think I will probably die of AIDS," he blurted out. "Won't you?"

Yes, I expect so. In my gut, I know it. Yet in the back of my mind, I just can't believe it: Maybe, just maybe, I'll live to see a treatment breakthrough.

How different these AIDS interviews now are from the one four years ago with the Rays, when all was well and I was just a spectator to the train wreck, not riding in one of the cars. It was simple then: A quick good-bye. A shake of the hand. A perfunctory wish for the future. Then off into the night. Now, it's embraces and tears and whispers from me and for me: "Stay well," "Don't give up," "God bless." And always there is that one futile question: Have you found the magic cure?

To have AIDS is to be alone, no matter the number of friends and family members around. Then, to be with someone who has H.I.V.—be it interviewer or interviewee—is to find kinship. "I'm so glad they picked you to do this," Mary Fisher said in an interview just before she spoke at the Republican National Convention as a woman with H.I.V. With her, as with Magic Johnson and Bob Hattoy and Larry Kramer and Elizabeth Glaser, who spoke at the Democratic convention, the talk was the same: of anger and courage and politics. We talked of that deep nausea in the pit of your stomach when even cancer patients pity you and when a doctor, who should know better, puts on latex gloves just to shake your hand.

There are time-outs in each of the interviews for both of us to get tissues, for both to pop our AZT, for both to laugh and always to hug. "I will see you again," Magic Johnson said pointedly, in what was not a social nicety but an affirmation of life between two people with H.I.V. Like each of the other interviews, ours was therapy for him. It was therapy for me.

"Who are you?" a TV reporter asked me at a funeral march in Greenwich Village for an Act-Up leader dead of AIDS. The reporter knew full well who I was: the guy from The Times with AIDS.

The lid of the coffin had been removed, the open box carried on shoulders in the rain, led in the dusk by mourners with torches, the dirge of a single drumbeat setting the pace of this, a funeral turned protest against President Bush's handling of AIDS.

"Are you here as a reporter or as a gay man with AIDS?" the TV correspondent persisted, shoving a microphone in my face. His camera spotlight went on.

I didn't respond. People in the crowd moved closer; they wanted to know the answer. I wanted to know it, too. Finally, it came out: "Reporter." Some shook their heads in disgust, all but shouting "Uncle Tom!" They wanted an advocate, not a reporter. So there I stood, a gay man with AIDS out of place at an AIDS funeral, an outsider in my own world.

I walked back to the office in the rain, thinking along the 30 blocks about how tough it must be for blacks to report about blacks, for women to report about women. Yet that kind of reporting is the cutting edge of journalism. Some people think it is the journalism that suffers, that objectivity is abandoned. But they are wrong. If the reporters have any integrity at all, it is they who suffer, caught between two allegiances.

Don't misunderstand; it was I, not my editors, who pressed for me to write about AIDS. For 20 years, I had been a by-the-book Timesman, no personal involvement allowed. But now I see the world through the prism of AIDS. I feel an obligation to those with AIDS to write about it and an obligation to the newspaper to write what just about no other reporter in America can cover in quite the same way. And I feel an obligation to myself. This is the place—reporting—where I am at home. This is the place where I must come to terms with AIDS.

I didn't write an article about the funeral march, judging it worth only a picture and a caption. I passed the journalism test that afternoon in the rain by failing the activism test. To turn activist would mean that AIDS, not reporting, would define me. It would be to surrender totally to the disease.

But no matter how neatly it works out in the mind, that doesn't make it any easier, even when I'm reporting on issues besides AIDS.

Traveling the country to interview voters about the Presidential election, I dropped by an Iowa cafe where, as a reporter from New York, I was hailed as a mini-celebrity.

Asked to say a few words at a breakfast of 30 leading citizens, I wanted to tell them I had AIDS, to watch the stunned look on their faces. But I didn't. That would have crossed the line between reporter and activist. Yet I do tell some politicians I interview. In my mind, that's O.K. I can't explain why. I left the breakfast in Iowa feeling hypocritical, a disciple who professes to carry the message of AIDS but is most comfortable preaching to the converted.

"Why are you here with me?" Jerry Brown asked when, while I was covering his Presidential campaign for a few days, the conversation turned to AIDS and I told him that I had it. "I'm here," I said, "because it is what I do."

He leaned closer to me, asking quietly, "Don't you want to be off getting in touch with your spirituality?"

Religion. How I have wrestled with that one. I had wanted to stop in church the day before brain surgery. But to me it would have been the height of hypocrisy to turn to God in desperation after years of turning away.

Yet I have become more spiritual. I think often of the dozen friends who have died of AIDS, and I feel them with me. It's not that I am writing editorials, avenging their deaths. It's that I feel their strength, their soothing me on. They are my conscience, their shadows with me everywhere: In the torchlight of the march. Over my shoulder. By my desk. In my sleep.

On its surface, life is much the same as before: I walk into the newsroom, sit at my desk, work the phone. But it is a through-the-looking-glass world. Sitting in my doctor's office, listening to the latest update, I can't help thinking, "This is a good story."

An interview with Clinton on gay issues and AIDS was the oddest I've ever had. He had been briefed that I had the virus, but we never discussed it. It seemed self-centered for me to bring it up, and I guess he thought it rude for him to do it. So there we were, talking about AIDS. I knew that he knew that I knew that he knew.

Before me on the desk are the letters—a hundred of them this year, some from people who read that I had AIDS, others from people who figured it out between the lines of my pieces. Those are the ones that I am proudest of. "Consider this letter a giant hug," wrote a man from Philadelphia. I have killed the message on my phone tape from a man dying of AIDS who had called begging me to save his life, to give him some nugget of information that would keep him alive. "Please!" he cried. I called him back to say there was nothing I could do except recommend doctors. I kept that tape for weeks, playing it over and over. "Please!" I wonder if he is dead now.

Oh, I have come to understand the Rays—those people who seemed so glib. Now, I see that they are like all of us with AIDS, trying to go on about their lives but caught up in this nightmare. They do what they have to do. We all do. I think about them. I am one with them. And I think about Ricky, the newest shadow looking over my shoulder.

My editors keep an eye on me, I am sure, to make certain that AIDS has not yet weakened my reporting. But I suspect I will be the first to say when it is time to call it quits. As I write this, I feel tired but sharp. The AZT is holding for now. The brain infection, though diminished, is still present, making the fingers of my right hand stiff and clumsy on the keyboard. I use a tape recorder; my short-term memory isn't what it was.

I hold a different job—one that is supposed to be less stressful. But I am sitting in my old spot in the newsroom to finish this, the same spot where I suffered the seizure. As I look up, I can see the wall clock clearly. I couldn't that Dec. 21 when failing vision was the first sign of trouble. Now, two years later, I see things more clearly than ever. And I am alive.

That personal essay, more than even the totality of Jeff's profiles of other people with HIV or AIDS, brought him an unexpected, unbidden type of celebrity. There were TV shows, magazine features, speeches, photo shoots. However much the spotlight went against Jeff's longtime ethos—the story, not the reporter, is the story—he quickly realized the broader benefits that his temporal fame could bring to AIDS awareness and full acceptance of gays.

Wendy Schmalz Wilde

I think he enjoyed the celebrity to an extent. He often referred to himself as the poster boy for AIDS. He said that, "I've become the poster boy for AIDS." I think he liked being on the ABC show, *Day One*. He liked being on *Charlie Rose*. The Charlie Rose interview is hysterical because of the Magic Johnson references. Jeff kept saying, "It's hard to separate Magic Johnson from baseball. Baseball is his life." Charlie Rose said, "Basketball," and Jeff's like, "Yeah, okay, basketball." The interview goes on, and about ten or fifteen minutes later, he goes, "So Magic Johnson and baseball. It's just there." Charlie Rose says, "Basketball," and Jeff's like, "Yeah, whatever."

There was just one terrible story. Annie Leibovitz was doing a photo spread on Jeff for *Vanity Fair*. Jeff always wore glasses. He wore glasses when he was two years old. He had contacts briefly, but he didn't like them. His glasses were such a part of him. He had his Paul Stuart shirts and his church shoes and everything was starched and pressed. She said, "I want you to look like a newsman. Take your glasses off and take your shirt off, rumple it up and put it back on." He did. Why he did this I don't know, because that's so not like him. I have a whole stack of these photos and I hate them, because they just are not Jeff at all. They are not even kind-of Jeff.

In the wake of his first-person article, Jeff was invited to speak at the Dalton School, an elite private high school in Manhattan, on February 16, 1993. At his request, rather than delivering a prepared speech, he fielded questions from students.

STUDENT

Why did you work?

JEFF SCHMALZ

Everybody has to respond to this in their own way. I was too sick to do anything. I was in the hospital six times in the first seven months after being diagnosed. I was also, I realize now, in a state of depression. It was such a shock. I thought about retiring and thought about going off to Europe or wherever or doing things I had never done. But to me, working was so much a part of my life and a part of who I am. I realized I was in a position very few people are in and I realized I could be an advocate and a voice for people who have AIDS. I returned to work and then really didn't do anything. I was so depressed I couldn't write. I started some pieces and then it was too depressing.

Then came the presidential race and I started to do that. And then, the more I did that, the more I started coming out of my depression and the more I started easing into some AIDS stories and I was very pleased with the response that I got. What was interesting about the outpouring was that readers sort of figured out I had AIDS. "We read that story and sensed that maybe you're HIV-positive." I felt I was getting my message across and I started writing more and more. And then I started making appearances like this, and, I must say, I do think often of just retiring and saying, that's enough already. It's hard emotionally and hard physically. I look robust, but I am tired by the end of the day. But I feel the need to press on.

I work every day, just about seven days a week . . . I work a pretty aggressive day. I'm in fairly early and I work into evening. I write a piece about every week or two weeks, which isn't a lot, but I write long pieces. One of the things I'm very worried about is that I don't want the quality of my work to start slipping. I'm worried that my mind might start to go and I may misperceive something or that I might get a quote wrong. When I finish a piece, I ask myself, "Is it time to give up?" because I don't want to compromise. I'm sure my editors will let me know. I will be the one to say it's time to let go, because my standards are high and I really don't want to compromise the paper.

STUDENT

Do you feel cheated?

JEFF SCHMALZ

When you think you're going to die and then you live—and not just live but thrive—you don't feel cheated. You feel blessed. I don't stand before you as someone who feels cheated. I stand before you as someone who was given time—a year now that I never thought I'd have. Time that I've been able to put to really good use. I'm proud of that. Not only to write about AIDS. But time to get my life in order.

During the early months of 1993, Jeff bought a co-op apartment near Lincoln Center, finally giving up the small place on the Upper West Side from his student days at Columbia. He would also fall in love with Louis Broman, whom he met in an AIDS support group. This was Jeff's first domestic relationship since living with an older architect in his early years in New York. Even while sick, Jeff exuded a life force that struck friends and family.

Adam Moss

He whistled. You'd always know he's coming around the corner because you heard the sound of his whistle. Every morning, every day when he'd come back from lunch, he was one of the happier-seeming people. Here's this person who has what he believes and eventually was right to believe is a fatal disease and yet something had opened him up. Something had given his life a certain kind of joy at the same time. It was incredibly poignant and very vivid and sort of shocking to see. I didn't know the old Jeff. I didn't know the buttoned-down Jeff. I know that Jeff only from his own telling. I just knew this new Jeff, who felt, I think, so relieved not to be carrying secrets, not to be having to perform the function of a *Times* man.

David Dunlap

At a time when Jeff was quite sick but still mobile, Jeff went with me and my partner Roy to a theater in the East Village to see *Paris Is Burning*. It is a delightful movie and ultimately a poignant and very sad movie about voguing and the various houses who compete with one another with these fantastic fashion poses. It's kind of the emulation by black and Latino gay subculture of *Vogue* magazine and high fashion. We come out of the theater at midnight and are headed back to the Upper West Side, where Jeff also lives. We wanted to share a cab back. Jeff says, "No, the evening is young." We sort of look at him and at one another and he says, "I may be sick, but I'm not dead." He walked off into the East Village night for some fresh sexual conquest.

Wendy Schmalz Wilde

Jeff said something terrible about Cuomo in the *Post* Page Six [gossip column]. I don't remember what it was. Cuomo called him up and said, "I'm going to sue you. You're going to be sorry." Jeff said, "Fine, sue a man dying of AIDS. See what that gets you."

David Dunlap

During Jeff's last year, this man who had, as the cliché goes, a steel-trap mind was suddenly forgetting things and sort of losing his way mid-sentence or mid-paragraph. He was laughing it off, but there was a slowness to Jeff, a cloudiness coming over him. There was a general sense among his friends that his mental faculties were increasingly impaired.

Shortly before Jeff really had to leave *The Times* in the fall of 1993, we had lunch and it was not his usual snap, crackle, and pop of conversation. But it was a fond and friendly lunch. And I have a very vivid memory of walking east on the north side of 43rd Street on a sunny day back toward *The Times'* headquarters. Jeff had his arm through mine, partly out of fondness and perhaps out of just physical support to help keep him steady.

I remember thinking, "Oh, my God, I'm walking arm-in-arm with another man toward *The New York Times* building," and having that old sense of fear of what if they see me? Who is they? Everyone knows I'm gay, but what if they see me? I almost said, "No, Jeff, we're getting too close to the building. It's okay by 8th Avenue, but we're getting too close to the entrance. Let's unlock here." It was clear that he wanted to stay arms locked until we had to negotiate the revolving door. Then I felt that sense of, "No stay with it. Cherish this man. Hold him tight."

Jeff grew up in Walnut Grove, Pa. – this is his high school graduation photo – but he desperately wanted to get out and live in New York, especially as he came to realize in his teenaged years that he was gay. Photo courtesy of Wendy Schmalz Wilde.

Jeff's editing talent was recognized early in his years on *The Times*. In the summer of 1975, when he was only 21, he was put on the team that revised the newspaper's authoritative and influential *Style Book*. From left to right: Jeff, Eileen Butler, Allan Siegal and Lou Jordan, the news editor who oversaw the project. Photo by Teresa Zabala/*The New York Times*.

Although Jeff never held the title of metropolitan editor, he essentially ran *The Times'* city and suburban coverage in the late 1970s and early 1980s. Here he is among the metro desk staff in 1982. Left to right: William Greer, Jeff, Nicholas Horrock, Charles Strum, Dennis Stern, James Gleick. Photo courtesy of New York Times Company Archives.

With *The Times* as his surrogate home, Jeff's work life and social life often overlapped. Here he picnics in the early 1980s with friends and colleagues including Anna Quindlen (second from left) and Arthur Sulzberger, Jr. (center). Photo courtesy of Ben Kushner.

Having already excelled as an editor, Jeff began to build his reputation as a tough and incisive reporter while serving at *The Times*' bureau chief in Albany. There he often tangled with New York's idealistic but thin-skinned governor, Mario Cuomo. They strike a relatively civil pose here at the Legislative Correspondents Association dinner in 1988. Photo courtesy of Wendy Schmalz Wilde.

> **Buy Your Lies Here.**
>
> # THE NEW YORK TIMES REPORTS HALF THE TRUTH ABOUT AIDS.
>
> **ACT UP. FIGHT BACK. FIGHT AIDS.**

ACT UP, the group of militant AIDS activists led by Larry Kramer, relentlessly criticized *The Times* for alleged deficiencies in its AIDS coverage. The flyer, from about 1990, was typical in its bold tone. Flyer reprinted with permission of ACT UP New York records. Manuscripts and Archives Division. The New York Public Library. Astor, Lenox, and Tilden Foundations.

Once Jeff took on the AIDS beat, he struggled to strike a balance between journalism and activism on the subject. Here he joined *The New York Times* contingent for the AIDS Walk in 1993. Back row left to right: Lynda Richardson, Richard Meislin, Jeff, Roy Finamore, Michael Wilde. Front row left to right: Ben Kushner, David Dunlap, Hendrik Uyttendaele, Wendy Schmalz Wilde. Photo courtesy of Wendy Schmalz Wilde.

Jeff covered AIDS during the final year and a half of his life. At his desk in the newsroom during that period, he is as dapper as ever in his bow tie but visibly drained by the disease that would kill him at age 39. Photo courtesy of Ben Kushner.

PART THREE: LEGACY

Mary Fisher

After the election and into the Clinton Administration in 1993, Jeffrey Schmalz and I had become close friends. Among other things, he became my most faithful speech reader. When Jim [Heynen, her close associate] sent me a first draft, I sent a copy to Jeffrey for his reactions. He rarely suggested changes, but he told me over dinner in May that my voice had changed since Arthur's death.[1] He thought I was more introspective, sadder, and angrier. "Where do you go with all of that?" I asked. He had been in the middle of this epidemic for a decade. He had lost hundreds of friends. He had filed more than 1,000 stories[2] on AIDS—grim stories, sometimes brutally depressing, sometimes heartbreaking. "There's no place to put this, Mary," he said, "except where you're putting it now, in your speeches. Feel the pain and tell others. What else is there?"

---

1 Arthur Ashe, the tennis star, died on AIDS on February 6, 1993.
2 Jeff Schmalz wrote about 40 articles on AIDS, though their impact made the body of work seem much larger.

In April 1993, Jeff traveled to San Francisco to interview Randy Shilts, who was a kind of role model. He had come out more than a decade before Jeff and he had begun covering AIDS in the early 1980s. His 1987 book, And The Band Played On, *was instantly hailed as the definitive account of the epidemic. On the day when Shilts finished the manuscript, he was diagnosed with HIV. By the time Jeff interviewed him, he was severely ill with full-blown AIDS. While the news peg for the article was the release of Shilts's new book* Conduct Unbecoming, *a history of gays in the American military, the presentiment of death pervaded Jeff's prose.*

April 22, 1993

AT HOME WITH: RANDY SHILTS;

WRITING AGAINST TIME, VALIANTLY

By JEFFREY SCHMALZ

These should be the best of times for Randy Shilts. His new book, "Conduct Unbecoming," is hitting stores now, a portrait of homosexuals in the military coming as the issue seizes the country's conscience. A movie based on his first book, "The Mayor of Castro Street," published in 1982, is about to go into production. An HBO film of his second book, "And the Band Played On," just finished shooting. He has a 23-year-old boyfriend (Barry Barbieri), a 10-acre retreat in the country, even a trusty dog (Dashiel).

But Mr. Shilts, 41, who was made famous by his writing on AIDS, has himself developed AIDS, and it is wearing him down. He comes to the door of his apartment here tethered to an oxygen tank, the legacy of a collapsed lung not yet healed. One minute he is the old Randy Shilts, a blur of energy and issues and passion, musing over the possibility of a new book, railing against the abuse of gay and lesbian Americans in the military. The next, he isn't Randy Shilts at all. He's just another gay man with AIDS, scared and tired, trading gossip about the newest drugs and monitoring the declining level of white blood cells that support his immune system—his T-cell count.

"H.I.V. is certainly character-building," he says, easing his breathing by reclining on the sofa. "It's made me see all of the shallow things we cling to, like ego and vanity." Not missing a beat, he adds, "Of course, I'd rather have a few more T-cells and a little less character."

. . . In the end, writing the book almost killed him. He started research in 1988—unsure of whether there would be any broad interest in such a book—but wrote most of it last year. He was supposed to have inhaled aerosolized pentamidine to protect against pneumonia. But he got so caught up in his writing that he didn't want to leave the cabin and come to San Francisco once a month for the relatively simple treatment. "I should have known better," he says.

Sure enough, last August, he contracted pneumocystis carinii pneumonia, crossing the threshold from being H.I.V. positive to having full-blown AIDS. He got pneumocystis again in December. On Christmas Eve, a lung collapsed. What followed was a seven-week life-and-death battle—surgery, even a ventilator. "I almost gave up and died six weeks ago," he says. The last paragraphs of "Conduct Unbecoming" were dictated from his hospital bed . . .

Mr. Shilts, who took AZT for five years until it lost its effectiveness and is now not on any antiviral medication, walks slowly as he gives a tour of the apartment. At times short of breath, at other times strong, he often seems just plain weary.

"Straight people," he says, "should be giving awards to those of us with AIDS who go on being productive members of society."

Just the day before, he had been found to have kaposi's sarcoma, the AIDS-releated cancer that causes purplish lesions. He got the diagnosis from Marcus Conant, the very doctor whom Mr. Shilts had followed in "Band" as he diagnosed K.S. in one patient after another. Randy Shilts has become one of the people he wrote about.

. . . "I have to take care of myself," he says. "Another thing could knock me out. I can't get pneumonia again." Then he comes back to the conversation: "Yeah, I have a good life. I'd be happier if I didn't have to worry about dying."

On June 17, 1993, The New York Times published a profile of the novelist Harold Brodkey, who had recently been diagnosed with AIDS. This would be the last time for more than five months that the words BY JEFFREY SCHMALZ appeared in print. Meanwhile, the ABC television news-magazine show Day One *began preparing a segment about Jeff. He was interviewed for it in his apartment on July 22, 1993.*

Forrest Sawyer: As time grows shorter, do you feel pulled to be an activist?

Schmalz: I feel myself getting angrier. I understand the rage of ACT UP. I don't always agree with their tactics, but I understand their rage. I mean, my God, we're dying here. When you talk to officials . . . they are all sympathetic. "There, there. If we were dying, we'd be angry, too. We're working on this and somewhere down the road, we may have a cure." That's fine, but I don't have some years down the road. My time of crisis is now—this second, this minute. I'm not hearing government say that and seeing government take steps that reflect that.

Now, is that activist? Maybe. Yeah. If so, fine. I'm also a gay man with AIDS and I'm angry and I'm frustrated. I wish more was being done. Having said that, I do not subscribe to the line that's being put out there by Larry Kramer and others that Bill Clinton is a disaster on AIDS. I think he's done wonderful things on increasing money. What we have is a blind rage at the virus. I'm sorry I'm dying of AIDS. I'm angry and I'm angry at the world. I'm not necessarily angry to Democrat or Republican or Clinton or Reagan. I'm just angry and I want help. Is that political? Maybe yes, maybe no.

During this same period of time, Jeff was putting the dynamic tension he felt—between journalist and activist, chronicler and victim—into a lengthy article for The New York Times Magazine.

Adam Moss

Jeff and I had been talking over time and eventually I went to the magazine, first as a consultant and then as the editorial director. We were talking sometime in 1993 and he uttered the phrase, "Whatever happened to AIDS?" I said to him, "That's a magazine article." I tried to convince him that the way for him to do the magazine article was to do it in the first-person and then as a first-person narrator try to also inhabit the role of a reporter and to try to fuse these two things. He was very excited by the prospect but also extremely nervous. It went against all of his journalistic instincts at the time. I don't remember when he first started the article, but it was way, way, way before the story was eventually finished and published.

The story was written in spurts. He would write a sort of furious passage and then let me see that. That would be in one persona, the persona of the gay man with AIDS. And then, in the persona of the reporter, he would do very sober exposition and inquiry constructed around these various interviews he had with various people in medicine and politics and activism. It wasn't always the structure of the piece, but it became the structure of the piece, because it could sort of accommodate what he could do. He could get himself together to do this interview and he would have these more private explosions of rage. The problem was to figure out how to make that all one story. The problem was how to get Jeff comfortable with doing a story like this.

It became clear gradually in the way that these things work. He'd have good days and bad days. There was a hope that there would be enough good days to carry it through. Then eventually there was sort of nothing more to come out of him and one was torn as his editor and his friend, between wanting to push him to finish this thing that I felt was very important and that he felt was very important to him. I had to push him, yet not to push him, because there were clearly more important things happening to him, which is that he was sort of grappling with his end.

Adam Nagourney

Jeff was perceptive enough to realize that he just couldn't quite finish the article. He had trouble closing it. That was a sign to all of us that he was having cognitive difficulties. Normally, that'd be no problem for him.

Adam Moss was trying to figure out a way to sort of retrieve it and redeem it. It was all there, but because Jeff had lost a train of thought, it just needed some sharpening. I don't think Jeff would ever need a ghost-writer or a collaborator, but he needed someone to just bring it over the finish line.

Adam Moss

I can't remember whether Adam volunteered for this or whether I asked him or Jeff even asked him to do it. But there was a moment in which it was, "Okay, let's do this together. Let's make this piece work for Jeff together." Here are the obvious reporting holes that are still in the story. Here is this sort of narrative that needed to be stitched together. In the mean time, I'll take what Jeff wrote and try to put it in a structure that could accommodate the way he wrote and would still have the power that was really so evident in the language itself that was just Jeff. Adam Nagourney couldn't write that. I couldn't write that. That was Jeff. Adam went out and got that other information, the sort of expositional work that Jeff had been unable to do. Then we stitched it together as a story and put the title on it that was obvious, "Whatever Happened to AIDS?"

Adam Nagourney

It was a very sad period. I'm thinking that by now it's September and we all realized what was going on with him. We were spending more time with him. He couldn't talk. In some ways, he almost died twice.

He could hardly communicate, except with his eyes. There was just such a weight of sadness. But I knew this piece was really important to him and I thought it was critical to do whatever I could with Adam to get it done.

I don't recall what I did with the interviews. Odds are I would have done them by phone. We're coming close to the end of it and we need information. Jeff was such a huge influence to me and such a help to me as a journalist. It's hard to overstate what a big deal he was. Jeff was such an extraordinary writer and I couldn't have his voice. The responsibility was scary. But I did consider it a moral calling as much as a favor to a colleague. And I always wondered if I was up to it.

Adam Moss

Really, the thesis of the story is very simple, which is that a lot of the political wars had been won. It was no longer a function of getting funding for AIDS. AIDS had come up against a wall. That wall was the wall of science. With all of the money and all of the resources and sort of changed policies that had happened during this very alive period of AIDS activism, they were still stuck at this moment when they could not solve the disease in a way that they would just a few years later with the drug cocktails. Much of the story is about his own sense of—pessimism is almost too light a word for it—raging that this will never be solved and can't be solved. Raging that people are now bored with it, because understanding the way news works and understanding what gets people engaged is newness. By this point, you know his contention was that AIDS was a boring story, because it did not have the catharsis ending—that actually, in some way, would happen later.

By the time ABC broadcast its segment about Jeff on Day One *on October 11, 1993, he was homebound and barely able to speak. In the coming days, he was hospitalized again and accepted for experimental AIDS treatment. The circle of friends and relatives immediately around him took to calling themselves "The Mishpacha," the Yiddish word for family. Jeff's brother-in-law, Michael Wilde, began keeping a diary.*

> **Friday, 10/15:** news from Hal Gal about a restraint bib being used on Jeff in New York Hospital. Wendy goes ballistic and makes a scene at the hospital, which I miss, as my job at the moment is to procure a duck dinner from one of Jeff's favorite restaurants . . .
>
> Hal's gift of roses, long-neck stems floating in water near the light, above my head, sublime; transfiguring.
>
> **[Undated, but approximately 10/17]:** Very angry about being admitted to the hospital. Wendy fighting his fight. Jeff is fully aware of what is happening. Tendency (of hospital staff) to talk to someone in his condition as if he were 4

years old. He understands perfectly. Level of frustration so great.

Swallowing team. Falling down. Incontinence in the solarium. Adam: "It was humiliating and degrading and then I thought, Good. Shit on New York Hospital. Let them get down on their hands and knees and wipe it up. Poetic justice."

Breaks down in tears (Wendy's only seen him cry twice) when he's touched. Adam: "Bernie Weinraub sends you his love." Clutches Irving (a stuffed green frog that croaks) as tears roll down his cheeks.

"I want to write."

Nurse: He won't be able to.

Wendy: It's OK, he's a writer.

Fri. 10/22: Wendy shows up at Jeff's: Oscar [a household aid] screaming into the telephone, nurses boiling mad (Oscar feels that Jeff can get better, yelling "put your foot up! You can do it!" can't accept fact that Jeff won't get better). Jeff sitting at the table crying. Doorbell rings, Wendy opens the door: "Hi! I'm Mary Fisher!" bags in hand, straight from the airport. "Here are some flowers."

Mary Fisher

We were together for the last time. The virus was having its way with him. His speech was gone, so I spoke only to his eyes. I sat beside him, telling him that the children were well and that he had been very brave and that I loved him and he could let go now if he wanted to. In the silence of that room, he turned to me and said in a clear, steady voice, "Your eyes." They were, I suppose, full of grief and perhaps comfort.

Michael Wilde's diary continues.

10/25: Wendy having to fight the nurse service not to restrain him in his own bed. Jeff mechanically rubbing his arm, bored, angry. Imagine running warm water over a handful of ice cubes; soon you're left with nothing but water slipping through fingers.

10/26: His writing with pencil and paper: *This is odious. Dying is monstrous.*

10/27: Jeff wrote *Injustice* and *Soon*—underlined and stared at Wendy. Then *Soon* and stared at Wendy again. Wendy: "Jeff I know it'll be soon"—and that seemed to calm him down."

10/30: Dinner at J's. Taking antipsychotic med. (Ladd Spiegel thinks he may be hallucinating.) Compulsive repetitive head scratching, rubbing of a single spot, scraping of bowl when food is gone, etc., continual shaking of right leg. We sat around the fire (the first of the season), I sang one too many verses of "Mr. Ed." and Wendy got mad.

11/3: Rapid decline. High fever. Very high blood pressure (170/ 120). Moving arm up and down while holding hands compulsively. W got in bed with J and he held her hand w/vicelike grip. Sunken eyes, protruding cheekbones, protruding teeth, and deathmask.

11/5: Friday night. Fever 105 (and climbing), Tylenol suppositories ineffective. I don't think he'll last the night. W Adam and Ben (and Nurse) w/J. Sleepless night for me. I woke up at an unknown hour wondering if he's alive. My dream: Jeff's fever breaks, he unwinds towels from his head and speaks eloquently, joking, some slurring of words but "better."

Richard Meislin

The last time I saw him was the evening before he died. He had a penthouse apartment in the 60s. He was in bed and there were a number of friends around. Mostly, he was not conscious. It was clear that we were coming to the end.

A very strange feeling about the whole thing for me was that I had written his obituary in advance, since we knew this was not that far away. Harold Gal, who was then the obituary editor and also a friend of Jeff's, had come up to me a number of weeks earlier and asked me whether I would do it, even though I was the graphics editor at the time. I said, "Yes."

I did not interview Jeff for it. But I knew him well enough and we had talked about the things that would make sense to put in. In general over the years we had talked about things that would make obvious sense to put in his obituary. There wasn't a need for a separate interview.

It turned out to be an incredibly difficult task to do. I don't advise writing the obituary for a friend of yours, because in some sense you have to put it in your brain that you're writing this in the past tense, and it's a very hard thing to do.

David Dunlap

In the very final weeks of Jeff's life, I found myself admitted or readmitted to the innermost circle of friends and family—in no small measure because I lived about six blocks away. I was one of the people who could be counted on at those dire moments to just get there. Adam Nagourney and his partner Ben Kushner were key as, of course, were Wendy and her husband.

Throughout that period, I would get calls—"This may be the moment"—and I would go to the house. I remember the last encounter with Jeff when there was a semblance of consciousness. The most amazing, touching, inevitable, inexplicable gesture. He's in the living room and must have been seated. I'm bending over him and he raises one crooked finger and I see it. It's kind of looking for my face. I don't even know whether he can see at this point but the finger sort of finds my forehead and he just held it there for a moment. It was that kind of inarticulate conversation you have with those who are about to die where they're clearly moving already to another plane.

Then the morning came with the last call. I think Adam and Benj were already in the apartment fixing breakfast. They may have stayed there overnight. And there was a nurse there and Wendy was there. Her husband was there. We're in the bedroom. The bedroom is filled with light. We all kind of gather around Jeff. The nurse is helping us all because this is a new experience. Amazingly, Jeff is the only one of any of my friends who died of AIDS in whose company I was at the moment of death. I recall having my left arm under Jeff's shoulder and head so that he was cradled in the crook of my left elbow. I'm not sure where everyone is around that scene, but it's almost like the nativity scene in reverse. There's this figure in blankets and the rest of us around him. Basically, as you do with the dying, we're saying, "It's all right. It's all right. You can let go. You've had such a great run."

Jeff did have a life force, so you knew or inferred that there was still that part saying, "Goddamn it, I'm going to hang on." Our job was simply to say, "We love you. We're all around you. You can go. You can go now. You've done your job. You did it beautifully and you've got love everywhere around you." I think there was sort of a gargling breath that then simply stopped. Ben got up to open the window. That was the end. Then all of the things that you do began to kick in—the calls and the coroner and the removal of the body.

Wendy Schmalz Wilde

In Jeff's will, it says, "Under no circumstances am I to be buried in the family plot in Willow Grove, Pennsylvania." He'd first said that to me the night he told me he had AIDS. He said, "I don't want to buried there. Don't bury me there. I want my ashes scattered wherever you want. Just don't bury me there." He didn't want to go home again.

Michael Wilde's diary continues.

11/13: Scattering the ashes. 6:30 a.m. at the Christopher St. pier on West St., what Jeff jokingly referred to as "the scene of the crime."—What had once been the site of Bacchanalian roistering throughout the 70s and 80s is now desolate, a memorial to the dead and dying. The front of the pier is covered with names and poetry (for the most part mediocre), along with neo-Nazi hate graffiti ("Kill the gay-basterds") and stencils ("My beloved was queerbashed here"). Bright red and yellow spray paint bears the legend: AIDS MEMORIAL...

It's a long walk to the end of the pier. Beautiful morning. Luckily, a north-westerly wind. Gray skies now. The somber moment approaches, and I can feel terror grip Wendy's heart. The tin is opened, and we discover the remains of Jeff in a plastic bag. Ben opens this with a Swiss army knife, and Rich attempts to stretch the bag around the edge of the tin, without success. "This isn't what you'd call user-friendly." He peers into the can and describes the contents as "gravelly." The time has arrived; a sober silence is observed, and Jeff is scattered to the wind.

Wendy, sobbing softly, bades farewell to her brother. Each of us, with a rose, tosses it gently into the river, and we stood and watched as the current carried him off, roses in tow, to the north. We stood silently and watched, until they disappeared. I turned and looked back toward the city, I'm not sure I know why. Maybe it seemed a different place to me. I looked at the Statue of Liberty, at the harbor, at the shanty town on the dock next to ours; I saw the Chrysler building, the Empire State Building, then back toward the roses. I looked at Ben's face, and saw quiet sorrow. The roses dipped in circling eddies, then they were gone. This wasn't Jeff the hero, it was just Jeff, and we were his family. For him it's over. Can I say the same for myself, or for Wendy, or for anyone else standing on that dock on this pleasant, dreary morning? The memory of his early death will forever be sad and bitter, even as grief subsides; there's no moral, no lesson. Only sorrow and regret.

On November 28, three weeks and one day after Jeff Schmalz died, his final article appeared in The New York Times *as the cover story of its magazine.*

WHATEVER HAPPENED TO AIDS?

By JEFFREY SCHMALZ

I have come to the realization that I will almost certainly die of AIDS. I have wavered on that point. When the disease was first diagnosed in early 1991, I was sure I would die—and soon. I was facing brain surgery; the surgeons discovered an infection often fates in four months. I would shortly develop pneumonia, than blood clots. I was hospitalized four times over five months. But by the end of that year, I thought differently. My health rebounded, almost certainly because of AZT. I was doing so well; I really might beat it. Now, it is clear I will not. You can beat the statistics only so long. My T-cell count, which was only 2 when I got my diagnosis, has never gone above 30—a dangerously low level. I have lived longer than the median survival time by 10 months. The treatments simply are not there. They are not even in the pipeline. A miracle is possible, of course. And for a long time, I though one would happen. But let's face it, a miracle isn't going to happen. One day soon I will simply become one of the 90 people in America to die that day of AIDS. It's like knowing I will be killed by a speeding car, but not knowing when or where.

I used to be an exception in my H.I.V. support group, the only one of its eight members who was not merely infected with the virus but who had advanced to full-blown AIDS. Now, just a year and a half later, the exception in my group is the one person who does not have AIDS. All the rest of us have deteriorated with the hallmarks of the disease—a seizure, Kaposi's sarcoma, pneumonia. Our weekly meetings simmer with desperation: We are getting sicker. I am getting sicker. Time is running out . . .

. . . Tim Bailey was one of the Marys, and that's as close to Act Up royalty as anybody can get.

The Marys are a subgroup of Act Up, the group involved in the more radical demonstrations, like disrupting services at St. Patrick's Cathedral. When Bailey died in June at 35, stipulating that he wanted a political funeral in Washington, Act Up was obliged to comply.

So on a drizzly Thursday at 7 A.M., two buses filled with Act Up members set out from New York. They were to rendezvous with the body in Washington, then carry the open coffin through the streets from the Capitol to the White House. They would show Bill Clinton the urgency of AIDS. They would bring one of its carcasses to his doorstep.

But it was not to be. The police would not let them march, and the day turned into a sodden fiasco, as the police and activists quarreled over the body, shoving the coffin in and out of a van parked in front of the Capitol. The rage was there, but the organization was not. And when the police said no, where did Act Up members run for help but the White House, the very target of their protest, getting Bob Hattoy, a White House staff member with AIDS, to intervene. In the end, Act Up members gave up and went home, taking the body with them.

It was a perfect metaphor for the state of AIDS activism—raging in desperate but unfocused anger, one foot on the inside, one on the outside . . .

. . . Still, as is so often the case with Bill Clinton, he is a victim of his own lofty campaign rhetoric. He spoke eloquently about AIDS in his pitches for the gay vote. He insisted that people infected with the AIDS virus, Bob Hattoy and Elizabeth Glaser, speak at the Democratic National Convention. On Election Night, he mentioned AIDS high in his victory speech. It all seemed so promising. David B. Mixner, a Clinton friend who helped rally the gay vote, exclaimed in the flush of a Clinton victory, "I believe thousands of my friends who wouldn't make it, who would die of AIDS, might make it now because Bill Clinton is President."

There it is: the man from Arkansas was to be not just President but savior. He's not. Bogged down early on in a battle over homosexuals in the military, Clinton has grown wary of anything that the public might perceive as a gay issue. He delayed fulfilling his campaign pledge to name an

AIDS czar, finally naming her five months into his term—and only when the National Commission on AIDS was about to attack him for not providing leadership on the epidemic.

More than anything else, what the AIDS community wants from Bill Clinton is a sense of urgency. . . "Other than myself, who lives with AIDS every day, there's no one at the White House for whom this is their first-tier issue," said Bob Hattoy, who, after serving six months as a White House aide often critical of the Administration's AIDS policies, was shifted to the Interior Department. He praised the President and Mrs. Clinton for having "a profoundly sensitive awareness about AIDS," but at the staff level, he said, "AIDS is not on the radar screens at the White House every day." And the political advisers? Hattoy scoffed. "I don't think they'll address AIDS until the Perot voters start getting it."

. . . AIDS, it seems, had become old news.

"In the early days of AIDS, when knowledge was expanding, there were lots of very compelling things to write about," said Marlene Cimons, who covers AIDS and Federal health policy out of the Washington bureau of The Los Angeles Times. "We were in the infant stages of making policy decisions about AIDS that had unique social and political ramifications. Now it's become harder to find angles.

We've written to death most aspects of the disease: AIDS in the classroom. AIDS in the workplace. Testing. They filled the front pages. Now there's a vacuum."

Stuart Shear, a reporter for "The MacNeil/Lehrer Newshour" who covers AIDS, said the conflicts that had made for good stories—the fights between Republican Administrations and AIDS advocates—were gone.

"It's become a pure science story," he said. "When it gets down to the clinical nitty-gritty, that's not what we look at. It's hard to get people to come on and complain about an Administration that's increasing funding." . . .

. . . The letters pour in from readers who know I have AIDS, which I wrote about in this newspaper last December. A Florida woman wrote detailing her son's agonizing death from AIDS. Halfway through the letter, she caught herself, suddenly blurting out, "I don't know why I am writing this to you." Like so many of the letters, it was really not so much for me as for the writer, an excuse to open up her heart and let out the pain. She ended with a line I think of often, a line as much for her dead son, also named Jeffrey, as for me. "I intend this letter," she wrote, "as a mother's hug."

Hardly a day goes by without my getting a letter or call from someone who has the cure for AIDS. Many are crackpots. But others, I'm not so sure. Perhaps I will soon be desperate enough to pursue them.

More and more of the letters are nasty, even cruel. They are still the minority, but they make clear how deep the resentment runs against the attention given AIDS.

"As an average American," a man from Brooklyn wrote in a letter to the editor that made its way to me, "I cannot feel compassion for those who contracted AIDS through the pleasures of homosexuality, promiscuity or drug injection. The advent of the AIDS sickness in the world breaks my heart—but only for those who contracted it from blood transfusion, medical skin pricks or birth. The insipid news stories and other media accounts of AIDS pain, pneumonias and cancers attempt to reach me, but they only turn me off. And I, in turn, turn them off, as I suppose that millions of your readers do. Let's permit these pleasure seekers of the flesh to live out their years in hospices or homes at minimal cost and then die."

Am I bitter? Increasingly, yes. At the Act Up funeral for Bailey in Washington, I thought of how much the anger of the activists mirrored my own. I, too, wanted to shout—at no one really, just to vent the rage. I am dying. Why doesn't someone help us?

I didn't shout. I couldn't. All I could think about on that rainy Thursday afternoon was that a political funeral is not for me. It is at once very noble and very tacky.

What, then, is for me? I usually say that my epitaph is not a phrase but the body of my work. I am writing it with each article, including this one. But actually, there is a phrase that I want shouted at my funeral and written on the memorial cards, a phrase that captures the mix of cynicism and despair that I feel right now and that I will almost certainly take to my grave: Whatever happened to AIDS?

On December 1, three days after the article appeared, President Clinton spoke on the occasion of World AIDS Day.

On Sunday, the cover story in the *New York Times* Sunday magazine was written by a journalist named Jeffrey Schmalz, who lived and just a couple of weeks ago died with AIDS. He was a remarkable man who interviewed me in a very piercing way when I was running for president. I was impressed then with the totally frank, almost brutal, and unsentimental nature of the interview in which we engaged and with the quality of his mind and spirit and the precision of his questions.

If you saw the article or you heard about it, you know that basically what the article said was AIDS is sort of receding in the public consciousness as a thing to be passionate about, that it was true not only in our administration but in the community at large and even in the gay community.

That was the theory of the article. And I think he was saying that people were just frustrated dealing with what they considered to be a perpetually uphill battle, not that it was politically unacceptable anymore to talk about AIDS or deal with it but that there just seemed to be no pay-off. And so he challenged us all with these words in the article, "I am dying. Why doesn't someone help us?"

I have to say to you that I think that is a good question and a good challenge. I do believe that all of us, each in our own way, sometimes just want to go on to other things. Even some of my friends who are infected just want to go on to other things—maybe especially them. They just get sick of talking about it and thinking about it and focusing on it.

The purpose of this day is to remind us that our attitudes, behavior, and passion should be revved up in the other 364 days of the year.

Two memorial services were held for Jeff Schmalz. The first, a dinner for his closest friends and colleagues, was held at his favorite restaurant, Chanterelle.

Wendy Schmalz Wilde

The service at Chanterelle was supposed to be the private one and when we got there, ACT UP was outside and they were picketing. The podium for the eulogizers was in front of this beautiful window.

It was nighttime and there were Christmas trees. ACT UP started throwing blood and eggs at the window behind the speakers. It infuriated me. I was livid. And it broke my heart.

The second service, a public event on December 7, took place at the Dalton School. Most of the speakers were Jeff's comrades and colleagues—Adam Nagourney, Anna Quindlen, Soma Behr Golden, Peter Kaufman, David Dunlap, Mary Fisher, Wendy Schmalz Wilde. Larry Kramer of ACT UP, Jeff's foil, also addressed the mourners.

Larry Kramer

I know that many do not welcome me here. I long ago became accustomed to being unwelcomed . . . I've been going to services like this for twelve years. I have no more tears left. I wanted to make a speech that would make you cry for the sadness of all this, but I can no longer even make myself cry. I'm empty inside. I'm not certain I can even feel anything anymore. All the Jeffs in my life are dead. All the bright, capable, talented hopes and dreams for our future have died . . .

Jeff died asking whatever happened to AIDS. He died asking you why he died. Have you asked yourself why he died? Does anyone who attends these endless memorials ever ask why did this person die? I mean why? Not what from, though that, too, but why. Have you asked yourself whatever happened to AIDS and put that together with why did Jeff die? Then, when you have asked yourself why, have you asked yourself the next big question? What did I do to help save Jeff's life?

You loved Jeff. You came here to mourn Jeff. Jeff died from a plague. What have you done to stop this plague? This plague that murdered Jeff, Jeff whom you came here to mourn. You probably didn't do very much because the plague is still raging and out of control and Jeff died. I guess you didn't do very much to help save his life, the life of the Jeff you say you loved and have come here to mourn. Why didn't you do anything? Why? . . .

Jeff may have worked for *The New York Times* but he was a member of one of the most oppressed minorities and AIDS is an evil act perpetrated on minorities. *The New York Times* could have saved Jeff, but it didn't. Since this plague began in 1981, it has chosen not to. Jeff was probably infected about that time. You came here to mourn him. If you cared about Jeff, then you are hypocrites if you continue to do nothing and continue to allow so little to be done and continue to allow the Jeffs of this world to die. A great many people in this room have enormous power. The newspaper that Jeff worked for has enormous power. What has that newspaper chosen to do with its power? Certainly not to fight to save the life of Jeff Schmalz, whom they claim to have loved.

I thought it was the moral responsibility of all of us to use what we are given to fight for the good of mankind. That's what every religion and philosophy commands. Did you? Did you do anything to save Jeff's life? No you didn't. Not really. I have come to hate almost everyone I know. AIDS has taught me how to do that. I hate you and yours for letting Jeff die, for allowing it to happen, for colluding in this genocide. If I hate you for this, then think of how much I hate myself even more, because in twelve years, no matter what I have said or how I have said it or where or to whom, I have not changed one goddamned thing. Please, in Jeff's name, use your power so that he will not have died in vain.

Adam Nagourney

I recently went back and looked at the video again of that event. I saw myself sitting next to Wendy, on the stage, holding programs. Larry made some very powerful and correct points about *The Times'* failures, ignoring AIDS coverage and gay issues for so many years. Nothing wrong with it, I get the point. But he was also doing stuff like, "You guys all killed Jeff." That was pretty intense. It was an uncomfortable moment, as you can imagine. I remember thinking, as Larry would do one more sentence, *Aren't we done yet?* I just looked down at the podium and pretended to talk to Wendy and point to something, as if we hadn't noticed what was going on at all. At the end of it, I thought Larry looked at me and Wendy. And I thought, *I learned something from covering politicians.*

Anna Quindlen

I followed Larry Kramer on the program at Dalton. In typical Larry Kramer fashion, he stood up and shrieked, "*The New York Times* killed Jeff. Everyone in this room killed Jeff." I hadn't been exposed to it very much, so that it came as a great surprise to me. It was just so preposterous.

As I was sitting there, I kept thinking that I don't want to respond to this. But Jeff would've said, "Too bad." I had my remarks prepared about Jeff, but it would have been preposterous for me to simply stand up and launch into my remarks. So I said something like, *"The New York Times* didn't kill Jeff. No one in this room killed Jeff. In fact, many of the people in this room loved and supported and helped him. AIDS killed Jeff. A virus killed Jeff." I just had to respond to it.

Her prepared remarks included this passage:

> Several months ago, I called Jeffrey for help with a letter I'd received from a reader; a 21-year-old man from a small, Southern town had come out he said for the first time, in a letter to me in which he explained that his girlfriend was pressing him for marriage. He said that most of the time he felt like being gay was this thing that he had to wrestle to the ground until it died the nasty death it deserved, but that every once in a while, he got a whiff through reading the paper of a world out there that thought differently. He wanted to know what advice I could give him before he decided to do what he described as "playing at being a married man." I felt wholly incapable of responding to that letter, so I called Jeff, who received letters like that all the time. We talked about it, and finally he said, "Look, you have to tell this guy the truth, that he can never really be happy until he acknowledges

openly who he is." Then there was a long silence as Jeff was pondering the depths of human nature. Finally he added, "You might also want to tell him how to get to the Castro."

The legacy of Jeff Schmalz was felt in the way American journalists for mainstream news organizations began to cover AIDS.

Michael Specter

Before Jeff, there weren't many people doing an AIDS beat. After Jeff, it was a rigorous beat at every place that was serious. That was all because of Jeff. Larry Kramer was a different kind of guy because he wasn't writing mainstream journalism. There were important loud people, but there was nobody like Jeff. He really did effect not just a generation of HIV reporting, but the way you write about disease now. You had people like Jeff saying, you can't write about a disease by doing what I often do, which is looking at the labs and talking to doctors. That's fine and you have to do it, but that's only part of it. The whole thing is, how does this affect a human being? How does it affect their family? How does it affect society? That didn't get written before.

Eric Marcus

Jeff was not the first journalist to report on his experience of having AIDS, not even close. The difference was that Jeff was at *The New York Times* and *The New York Times* is the paper of record. For example, Tom Cassidy at CNN, who was a business reporter and had a high profile, no one knows who he is any more. In April of 1990 he came out about having AIDS. He was so sick that he had to report it. He wound up in *People* magazine. He was interviewed on CNN. He was everywhere at the time talking about his experience. He talked about the importance of putting a face on AIDS. But he wasn't Jeff Schmalz. He wasn't at *The Times*. Jeff had been handed this unwanted gift to report on something from both the inside and the outside. He had the brilliance as a reporter and the position within *The New York Times* to do that. That's what made him so special. It was his unique sense of humor and his brilliant capacity to write and report.

Mary Fisher

Jeffrey moved the needle of sensitivity because of everyone he spoke about. He spoke about me, Magic Johnson, people in rural America and the gay community and those that were not in the gay community who were also affected and infected with this disease. I think that did bring a different look at what this disease was. I don't know whether he did it on purpose, but I think that it was fascinating to him, the wide swath that this epidemic was affecting. I think that his ability to focus on those people and bring it to a *New York Times* reader was amazing. I also think that it's amazing that *The Times* said, "Yes, go for it!"

Jeff Schmalz was not the first New York Times *journalist to die of AIDS. He had been preceded by a copy editor, Robert Barrios, and a writer, Lawrence Joseph. But because of the tremendous respect that*

Jeff commanded in the newsroom, his fight against the disease and his death from it exerted a profound influence on the newspaper's internal character and its coverage of AIDS and gay issues.

In a broader journalistic way, Jeff's work showed the powerful effect that first-person writing could have in The Times, *an institution traditionally wary of it. Again, he was not the first. Over a quarter-century before Jeff covered AIDS, A.M. Rosenthal, Nan Robertson, John Darnton, and Sydney Schanberg had written gripping, award-winning personal articles in the news columns on, respectively, the Nazi death camp at Auschwitz, toxic shock syndrome, the imposition of martial law in Poland, and the Khmer Rouge's genocidal conquest of Cambodia. In selectively breaking some of the rules he usually espoused—to be "down the middle," to use a "dead-away" tone—Jeff carried forth a style that would come to be called literary journalism or creative non-fiction.*

Adam Nagourney

In a weird way, one of the things that propelled the Gay Rights movement forward was AIDS, because it made a lot of people who otherwise would have been in the closet come out. They had no choice; they were sick and needed help, so all of the sudden, their parents, friends, relatives, and people at work realized they had gay people around them. That always has been the most powerful way to change the culture in terms of acceptance of gay people.

That's, I think, what happened to some extent at *The New York Times*. We had a couple of people out there—David Dunlap, Richard

Meislin and others—but when Jeff collapsed on the newsroom floor that day with a seizure that turned out to be AIDS, which we knew pretty quickly, all of the sudden there's this rising sorrow in *The New York Times*. It's hard to overstate what a big deal that was. I think it really had a lot to do with changing the culture of *The New York Times*. It was a classic example of how AIDS made the Gay Rights political movement make advances.

Arthur Sulzberger, Jr.

Jeff's stories pushed the envelope on opinion. But to be fair, that's part of what the magazine and the Week in Review were enabling journalists to do, to be a little more forthcoming about how a story affects you as the author and journalist. I think those were the right platforms for that kind of a story, so I think this was part of pushing the envelope for *The Times* in a healthy way. It's not commentary per se, but it's much more personal. We've grown that over the years since then. It takes a story and makes it not only intellectually engaging but engaging at the heart. There's such power to that. We remember those stories more than we remember any others. That's what Jeff gave us.

Richard Meislin

I think when young people hear about what *The Times* was like in the '70s and '80s and probably before that, they are just astonished. There was an event on the 15th floor maybe a year ago and it was marking some anniversary of the *Advocate*[3] piece, as I recall. Frank Bruni [an openly gay op-ed columnist] was on the panel and I was on the panel and a few other people. You could grasp from the response of the audience and some of the questions that the idea that things were hostile to gays not so very long ago was really startling. *The Times* has changed so much and has become such a force for equal treatment of gay and lesbian people that you would have had a very hard time imagining what it was like when I arrived here in 1975.

---

3   "Out At The New York Times: Gays, Lesbians, AIDS And Homophobia Inside America's Paper Of Record," by Michelangelo Signorile. Published May 5, 1992, in *The Advocate*.

David Dunlap

I look around the newsroom at the reporters and editors here who are cheerfully, openly, no-big-deal gay. And I am grateful for the very fact—which I used to resent—that no one knows what we fought against. Because I think that change is best that is no longer acknowledged. It's what these kids expect here. They don't know the history. The alter kocker in me wishes that some did and some cared about it, but it says more about this place that our struggle is now taken for granted than that it should be celebrated and any one of us should be ionized or held out as examples. Most of these kids don't even know who I am at this point. What young staffer knows the 62-year-old, 39-year veteran except as something that's in their way? And that's fine.

Anna Quindlen

I started writing columns about gay rights in 1990. I wrote an op-ed page column called "The Power of One." I almost did it accidentally. I hadn't really thought about gay rights. It wasn't a big issue on my radar screen. The response both pro and con and particularly pro from gay people saying, "I can't believe a straight woman is standing up for us in the pages of this paper." The responses were so fierce that I thought, this is my issue for now and forevermore. If anybody had told me then that if we fast-forwarded to 2014 we would be figuring out how many states let gay men and lesbians get married, I would have told them they were insane. The first time that there was a same-sex wedding announcement, I felt like the top of my head was going to blow off, because it was so at odds with what *The Times* had been like just ten or fifteen years before. It's been almost supersonic, the changes in American acceptance of gay men and lesbians as full citizens. Also the understanding that AIDS and HIV is no longer a death sentence, it's a chronic condition. So that when you rewind to where we were, it seems to have taken place in another country, in another era, in another century.

Mary Fisher

We have a very, very short attention span. I think Americans like the idea of the instant cure. The minute we said that there were medications, as you know, funding was drying up and people believed that it was over. There wasn't the fear created and there aren't people out there yelling and screaming about it now. I'm still talking and Larry Kramer's talking, but there aren't a lot of us out there who are actively explaining that this can still affect you if you don't use protection. People don't get it. And it's not so easy to take the medications. Not everybody can afford them. Not everyone can get access to them. It's not a cure. Yes, it's better. It's wonderful. Research has made it better, but it isn't the same. There's no fear around it, but it's still a fatal disease. People are still dying.

On March 25, 2013, as the Supreme Court prepared to hear the case involving California's Proposition 8 and the federal Defense of Marriage Act, The New York Times *published an editorial calling for a national right to marriage equality. Twenty years earlier, in one of his last half-dozen articles, Jeff Schmalz had written about the movement in Hawaii to enact same-sex marriage. It was the first such effort by any state. As* The Times *declared its position on the issue, the editorial page editor, who would have overseen if not personally written the editorial, was Andrew Rosenthal, the son of A.M. Rosenthal, the executive editor who had seemed to Jeff's generation to embody homophobia at the newspaper. Like Arthur Sulzberger, Jr., Andrew Rosenthal personified the transformative generational change on LGBT issues, both inside and outside* The New York Times.

A 50-STATE RULING

... The soundest approach is to recognize same-sex marriage broadly as a matter of equality under the Constitution—and therefore compel all states as well as the federal government to recognize this right. In the 2003 case Lawrence v. Texas, which struck down a Texas sodomy law as violating constitutionally protected liberty, Justice Anthony Kennedy, writing for the court, said, "As the Constitution endures, persons in every generation can invoke its principles in their own search for greater freedom."

Gay, lesbian, bisexual and transgender people have been seeking the freedom to live openly, to be treated equally and to marry as they choose. They have helped bring about a major shift in public opinion in the past decade in favor of same-sex marriage; they are now joined by leading Republicans and many of America's most import companies in making the powerful case for marriage equality before the court.

Support now for same-sex marriage—more than half in favor, about one-third against—is roughly the public divide on the question of public school desegregation in 1954 when the Supreme Court outlawed segregated schools in Brown v. Board of Education. But the court's call then for states to end racial discrimination in public schools "with all deliberate speed" was a big error. It gave states far too much latitude to move slowly and gave them an excuse for resistance, which delayed desegregation in many school districts for many years.

The court should avoid that kind of error in the same-sex-marriage cases. It should broadly declare that under the Constitution the right to marry applies equally to all couples, period, and that this principle applies to the federal government and every state.

With the growing tolerance of American society and the medical advances in treatment of AIDS, those who knew Jeff ruminate over the life he might have survived to lead.

Elizabeth Kolbert

I find myself thinking of Jeff in moments. I don't write on deadline very often anymore, but when I do and wish I had an unfiltered Camel, I think of Jeff. He always smoked unfiltered Camels and as the day went on in the Albany bureau, the smoke would start to emanate from our cave-like room. I remember one night when we were in the bureau and there was another reporter who had his first front-page story—I believe he was writing the lead of the paper—and was about to miss the eight o'clock deadline. I remember Jeff saying to him, "That's okay. We can just write 'Compliments of a Friend' there."

Richard Meislin

I have no doubt that, if Jeff had survived, he would have been a member of the masthead—the group of senior editors who basically run the paper. When I think about Jeff today, it still makes me sad that he had a lot of potential that went unrealized. I still sort of marvel at what he was able to accomplish during his last year or so in terms of really bringing attention in a startling and meaningful way to a disease and a social issue that really needed it.

Arthur Sulzberger, Jr.

Well, that's a wonderful question to ask. Unfortunately, it's almost impossible to answer, isn't it? He had enormous talent. Could I see Jeff having become an op-ed columnist for *The Times*? That would be possible. On the other hand, the managerial track was something that was also appealing. He came up those ranks a bit and then went into being a reporter. He could have gone back to those ranks. The joy of someone that talented is there's so many different opportunities. The question is, where would have his head been ten years later? Which path would he have wanted to go down?

Michael Specter

How can you relate to having your peers die? It was like watching people jump out of the World Trade Center one morning. You don't wake up on a really nice day in Manhattan and expect to see people just like you jumping out of the World Trade Center on fire. That's the way it was with AIDS—the idea that people just died at ages like 39.

I know a couple of people who got sick around the time that Jeff got sick. For genetic and biological reasons, HIV didn't eat away at their immune system radically, so they were able to carry on until there were effective drugs. They're fine. They take drugs every day the way people with diabetes and many other people in this country do. They are going to die of something else. It's like, if Jeff had gotten sick one year later. You think about that all of the time.

David Dunlap

Anyone who survived the epidemic, I suspect, has asked himself more than once, "Why did I survive?" If they are anything like me, they have no answer. As a practical matter, what I can say about those years of the '80s was that I was drinking heavily and in a paradoxical kind of way I think helped, because I was the kind of drinker who came from after work, opened a bottle of vodka from the freezer, put Jacques Brel albums on, clapped on the earphones, and just fell into this melancholy reverie and passed out in my chair and waited for the cat to wake me up the next morning because she was hungry. But we were all sitting under the sword of Damocles. The sword was just as bright and brilliant and pointed above my head as it was as Jeff's. I wasn't spending any time worrying whether Jeff had it. I was wondering whether I had it.

Michael Norman

When I first got to NYU as a professor in 1990, there were a couple of things that were missing that I never got over. One was a sense of common purpose and a close relationship between the people. I'd gone from the Marine Corps, where that was the case, to *The New York Times*, where it was definitely the case, to the academy, where it definitely was not the case. To express to my students that NYU is not the real fucking world, I put Jeff's obit up on my bulletin board in my office. Whenever something unpleasant, something disquieting happened in the academy, I would go to my office and look over at the photograph of Jeff's face and remember his lesson: *Get the job done and we'll talk about it later.*

You couldn't miss it. It was Jeff's obit and my Rutgers flag. I had a picture of Schmalz and a picture of Ernie Pyle during World War II.

I put them all up on a white board above my desk. And wouldn't you know that with 25 years of journalism students—an average of 30 a year, so 750 overall—not one, not one ever asked, "Who is that guy and why do you have him up there?" But it's as if Jeff was up there saying, *It doesn't matter. Just do the work.* This was a real fucking newsman, someone who knew the truth. If I could've written one word across Jeff's face, it would've been TRUTH.

AFTERWORD

Early on the Sunday afternoon of June 28, 2015, I stepped off a subway at the Christopher Street station and into a throng of celebrants inching up the stairs to the Pride Parade, which was passing literally above our heads. I had not attended the parade since covering it on assignment from Jeff Schmalz back in 1982, and the range and immensity of it all these years later stunned me. Where I recalled tens of thousands of marchers who were mostly young white gay men now I beheld an exponentially larger turnout: teenagers, senior citizens, Latinos, African-Americans, immigrants or immigrants' children from every continent. My wife and I somehow pressed our way across Seventh Avenue to the Stonewall Inn, the gay bar where a riot against police harassment in 1969 catalyzed the modern Gay Rights movement. This year, the cops were politely keeping order.

The buoyant mood attested to the Supreme Court's decision two days earlier to declare a Constitutional right to same-sex marriage. The grim motto of past marches, "Silence=Death," was replaced in 2015 by the joyous declaration, "Love Wins." Most remarkably of all, the deciding vote in the court's ruling for marriage equality had been cast by Justice Anthony Kennedy, a Roman Catholic who had been named to the court by Ronald Reagan.

Even for a middle-aged straight like me, or perhaps especially for a middle-aged straight like me, the pace of change was dazzling. My children had gone to school with classmates being raised by lesbian or gay couples. The son of one of my college buddies felt secure enough to come out in his public high school in Chicago. My son, by now 23, informed me that the marriage-equality ruling was great, of course, but marriage had been an easy issue. My daughter, who had just finished her junior year at Vassar, almost considered gays and lesbians old-fashioned compared to her queer or trans friends. What was that slightly disapproving term she used? Oh, right: cisgendered.

One part of me felt it necessary to remind my children just how recently gay people, much less gay marriage, had been a hugely divisive issue, ready fodder for bigots and demagogues. Decades of struggle had preceded that court decision. Another part of me, though, savored the sudden arrival of the new normal. And, of course, I fervently wished that Jeff Schmalz had lived to see it.

Jeff died less than two years before drug cocktails to control HIV and AIDS came onto the market. Some of the people he so memorably profiled—Mary Fisher, Magic Johnson, Larry Kramer—survived long enough to benefit from new treatments and lead vigorous lives to this day. Many others among Jeff's subjects, however, followed him into the grave. Randy Shilts died on February 17, 1994, at age 42. Elizabeth Glaser died on December 3, 1994, at age 47. Harold

Brodkey died on January 26, 1996, at age 65. Thomas Stoddard died on February 12, 1997, at age 48. Bob Hattoy died on March 4, 2007, at age 56. According to the Centers for Disease Control, more than 1.2 million Americans older than age 13 are currently infected with HIV and about 660,000 have died of AIDS in the 24 years of the epidemic. The battle, unlike marriage equality, has not yet been won.

Years ago, when I was working on a book about an African-American church, I often heard an aphorism about Jesus—that, by being resurrected, he "stole the victory from the grave." In telling and thus preserving the story of Jeff Schmalz, that grandiose phrase has echoed for me in a secular way. In little more than a year, at the very time he was dying, Jeff Schmalz produced a body of AIDS reporting that pierced the heart of readers and stirred the conscience of *The New York Times* in vital and lasting ways. If all this can be remembered, then not everything was scattered with his ashes.

GAYS IN JOURNALISM DURING THE AIDS YEARS: A TIMELINE

1977: Randy Shilts, who has already come out, is hired by KQED-TV in San Francisco. The *St. Paul Pioneer Press* runs an article with the headline: "Homo Hired to Be TV Reporter."

1979: Greg Brock, a news editor, comes out at the *Charlotte Observer*.

August 1981: Randy Shilts is hired by the *San Francisco Chronicle* just weeks after a new "gay disease" is detected.

1984: Greg Brock is hired by the *Washington Post*, making him the second openly gay person in the newsroom.

1987: On the day Randy Shilts turns in the manuscript for *And the Band Played On*, he finds out he's HIV-positive. He keeps that information secret.

1987: *The New York Times* amends its standard style to allow the word *gay* to be used as an ordinary adjective.

July 1988: Tom Cassidy, a business-news anchor for CNN, is diagnosed with AIDS. He keeps the diagnosis hidden.

October 11, 1988: Greg Brock, by this time the assistant managing editor for news on the *San Francisco Examiner*, appears on *Oprah* for the first National Coming Out Day.

April 1989: The American Society of Newspaper Editors (ASNE) authorizes its first-ever study of LGBT journalists in American newspapers. It is overseen by Roy Aarons, an editor at the *Oakland Tribune*.

April 1990: The survey—Alternatives: Gays and Lesbians in the Newsroom—is released at ASNE's national convention in Washington, D.C. Inspired by the report, LGBT journalists from across the United States and across media platforms express a desire to create a professional organization.

April 1990: Tom Cassidy of CNN discloses that he has AIDS.

December 1990: Jeff Schmalz has a brain seizure in *The New York Times* newsroom. Several months later, doctors determine that he has AIDS.

1991: Under Roy Aarons' guidance, the National Lesbian and Gay Journalists Association is officially incorporated and chapters begin forming throughout the country.

May 26, 1991: Tom Cassidy dies at age 41.

1993: Randy Shilts publicly discloses he has AIDS.

November 6, 1993: Jeff Schmalz dies at age 39.

February 17, 1994: Randy Shilts dies at age 42.

(Timeline courtesy of Eric Marcus.)

JEFF SCHMALZ COVERING AIDS: A SELECTED BIBLIOGRAPHY

"Riding AIDS Roller Coaster: Hope, Horror, Hope," June 6, 1992.

"Issues and Interests—Two Voices Speaking as One in Search of a Constituency to Combat AIDS," July 14, 1992.

"AIDS Test," August 16, 1992.

"A Delicate Balance: The Gay Vote; Gay Rights and AIDS Emerging As Divisive Issues in Campaign," August 20, 1992.

"Gay Politics Goes Mainstream," October 11, 1992.

"Gay Areas Are Jubilant Over Clinton," November 5, 1992.

"On the Book-Signing Circuit with Magic Johnson: Call Him Earvin: 'I Can't Be Magic,'" November 19, 1992.

"Covering AIDS And Living It: A Reporter's Testimony," December 20, 1992.

"Holidays and the Bad Tidings of H.I.V.," December 31, 1992.

"Homosexuals Wake to See a Referendum: It's on Them," January 31, 1993.

"On the Front Lines With: Joseph Steffan: From Midshipman To Gay Advocate," February 4, 1993.

"Gay Groups Regrouping For War on Military Ban," February 7, 1993.

"From Visions of Paradise to Hell on Earth," February 28, 1993.

"For Gay People, a Time of Triumph and Fear," March 7, 1993.

"At Home With: Randy Shilts: Writing Against Time, Valiantly," April 22, 1993.

"As Gay Marchers Gather, Mood Is Serious and Festive," April 25, 1993.

"Gay Marchers Throng Mall in Appeal for Rights," April 26, 1993.

"In Hawaii, Step Toward Legalized Gay Marriage," May 7, 1993.

"Fighting on 2 Levels; AIDS Institute Chief Has Disease," June 13, 1993.

"Two Documentaries, Two Different Takes on AIDS," June 13, 1993.

"Of Brodkey and AIDS: Laugh a Bit, Cry a Bit," June 17, 1993.

"Whatever Happened to AIDS?," November 28, 1993.

(All of these articles can be retrieved from www.nytimes.com)

INDEX

50-state ruling 156

ABC show 105, 125
ACT UP 55, 74, 79, 100, 118, 125, 139, 145
AIDS activism 139
   militant and confrontational form of 55
AIDS
   administration's staff focus on 141
   and Republicans 85, 141
   anger and frustration of patients/activists 125, 130, 139
   awareness 105
   casualty 59, 60, 63
   coverage 56, 75, 76
   definitive account on 122
   dying man's message 104
   epidemic, news coverage by *The New York Times* 38 *see also The New York Times*: gays and lesbians, institutional change towards
   grim stories on 121
   handling 89
   influence on life's vision 92, 93
   irrational fears on, legitimacy to 95
   Jeff Schmalz's work on 88, 96, 105
   life with 98-100
   misinformation in journalism industry 42
   people with, discrimination and abuse against 97
   public apathy 142, 143
   speech in democratic convention 82
   struggle to control 42
Anal intercourse 40

And the Band Played On see
    AIDS, definitive account on 107
Anti-gay people 78, 143
AZT 75, 100, 105, 124, 138

Bathhouses 41, 42
Break-up 21
Bush administration 55
Bush, President, handling of
    AIDS 101

Catholic church 55
Charlie Rose interview 106
Cities, with gay communities
    19, 20
Civil Rights movement 55
Clinton, Bill 72, 88, 90, 91,
    104, 121, 125, 126, 139, 140,
    143
Clinton—Jeff Schmalz meeting
    90
Closet 21, 28, 31, 34, 35, 43,
    53, 80, 152
Controversial issues, *NYT* method of dealing 26
Copy boys 22
Cuomo, Mario 57, 59, 110, 117

Democratic convention, speech
    on AIDS in 82, 85, 99
Depression, Jeff Schmalz's 71, 107
Discrimination against gay 38,
    40, 41, 50
"Drop beads" 31, 32

Ethics, professional 77
Food and Drug Administration
    64

Gay clubs 45
Gay communities, prominent
    cities with 19, 20
Gay community, growing clout
    of 72
Gay culture 42
Gay discrimination 38, 40, 41,
    50
Gay knitting circle 72
Gay men mindset 60
Gay Men's Health Crisis 44
Gay rights,
    country's view on 88
    political movement 152
Gay sexual behavior, measure
    and characterize 49
Gay teenager 18
Gay wedding announcements
    53, 155
Gay
    inhibitions for 30, 31, 35, 47
    acceptance of 105

getting connected 32
in American military 122, 140
Gossip column 110

Homophobia 37, 41, 156
Homosexuality, awareness of 46
Homosexuals, opportunities for 20

Jeff Schmalz —Clinton meeting 90
Jeff Schmalz,
    article on AIDS 96-105
    character, change in 80, 81, 106
    editorial ability 28, 129, 149-151
    end of (death) 135
    health condition, deteriorating 76, 110, 120, 127, 131-135
    humour 44
    last article 137
    mother, death of 71
    professional standard 108
    rise, through the ranks 26
    testing HIV-positive 70
Journalism, bad 57
Journalists, stuck between two allegiances 101

Marriage, same sex 52, 90, 156, 157
Military, American, gays in 122, 140

News, how it works 129, 141

Reagan administration 55
Republican politics 84, 85
Rosenthal, Abe,
    handling homosexuality issues 34, 37
    Pulitzer prize winner 28

Sexual escapades 94
Sexual habits 48
Shilts, Randy 122
Single-mother household 17
Sodomy law 156
Sulzberger Jr., Arthur, views on gays and lesbians 51, 52

T-cell count, measure of immune system health 69, 123
The 1962 Style Book 25
The Advocate 44
The New York Times,
    copy boy at 21
    coverage of AIDS 38, 39
    daring rarity in 96

failure of 146, 147
gays and lesbians, institu-
    tional change towards
    50, 53, 54, 152, 153, 156
Jeff Schmalz's ability 35

revising the style book 24
Tolerance, in American society
    158

World AIDS day 143

ACKNOWLEDGMENTS

This project began at a dinner with David Handelman and Syd Sidner, so it feels appropriate to start my litany of thanks with them. Their curiosity and enthusiasm began transforming my enduring obligation to Jeff Schmalz, and my unreconciled grief at his death, into journalistic form.

Wendy Schmalz Wilde, who barely knew me, took the leap of trust to agree to cooperate with my nascent idea for a radio documentary. At *The New York Times*, Arthur Sulzberger, Jr. provided essential personal and institutional support. And both Wendy and Arthur proved in their own interviews that they wanted a portrait of Jeff and *The Times* that was truthful, not air-brushed. The same can be said of all of the friends and coworkers of Jeff's whom we interviewed and who are listed at the front of this book. They all have my gratitude.

For more than a year, Kerry Donahue has been my partner and collaborator. I reached out to her for her exceptional talents as a radio producer, but in the course of our work together she became every bit as devoted to this story as I was. Kerry also brought into our circle the sound editor Ben Shapiro, John Barth of PRX, and Katie Kemple, a distribution consultant—all of them vital to the documentary's completion and dissemination.

Anthony Perrone at ABC News graciously allowed Kerry Donahue and me access to the research materials for the *Day One* segment about Jeff. Brandon Westerheim, Tal Nadan, and Kit Fluker of the New York Public Library helped guide me through the ACT UP archive. Eileen Murphy and Phyllis Collazo at *The Times* processed copyright licenses with great efficiency.

I am very fortunate to have known Tim Harper as a friend and fellow author, journalist, and educator for more than thirty years. In his current role as founding publisher of CUNY Journalism Press, he became an essential colleague in the Jeff Schmalz project, adding this book of oral history to CUNY's fine and growing list of titles. OR Books people—John Oakes, Emily Freyer, Matt Schantz, Justin Humphries, Courtney Andujar, Jen Overstreet, and Olga Rodriguez.

Besides Kerry and Tim, the project team included Kristofer Rios in social media and Web, Cathy Renna of Targetcue for publicity and promotion, and Christia Blomquist Freedman for graphic design and brand identity. Not so coincidentally, she is also my wife, my love, and the secret sharer in all my work. It is one of the greatest joys to be involved together in journalism as in all else.

Margot Atwell of Kickstarter was tremendously helpful and supportive in our successful fund-raising campaign. Sheila Coronel at Columbia Journalism School provided important start-up funding for Kerry Donahue. Jeff Roth, an archivist at *The Times*, and Ben

Kushner, a longtime friend of Jeff's, both contributed photographs that captured Jeff in his vigorous life. Beth Card was the epitome of alacrity and accuracy in transcribing our many, many hours of recorded interviews.

Barney Karpfinger, my literary agent and more importantly my friend, negotiated the contract for this book gratis—his own valuable contribution to the cause. Barney's life partner Eric Marcus, an exceptional historian of the LGBT experience in America, added important context to Jeff Schmalz's personal story. Jim Heynen and Mary Fisher lent their credibility in the fields of AIDS activism and philanthropy to this project.

S.G.F.

August 28, 2015

OUR BENEFACTORS

The majority of the funding for *Dying Words* – in the forms of this book and the companion radio documentary – came from donors to our Kickstarter campaign. Several individuals also made direct gifts. We thank all of them for their generosity and their belief in the importance of this project.

A full list of donors can be found on the website dyingwordsproject.com. Here we would like to single out those supporters who gave at especially high levels.

FEATURES EDITOR, $150-$249
Alice Alexiou, Ariane B. Lisa Belkin, Susan Carney, Ronald Figueroa, Ken Freedman, Stuart Freedman, Sarah Halevi, Elizabeth Kolbert, Bernadette Kriftcher, Tal Kra-oz, David Lewis, Kelly McMasters, Laura Muha, Adam Nagourney, Liz Nealon, Lynne Pate, Riv-Ellen Prell and Steven Foldes, Wendy Schmalz, Michael Schudson, Michael Shapiro, Amy Solas, James Tedrick, Brad Tuttle, Vball coach, Jake Walloch, Kerry Weber

NATIONAL EDITOR, $250-$349
Morris Allen, Alli and Colin Decker, Jim Ducayet, Margaret Ducayet, David Handelman, Shirley Idelson, Michael Janofsky, Steve Rago, Ruth Salzman, Marion Roach Smith, Gerald and Viviana Zelizer

COLUMNIST, $350-$499
Shifra Bronznick, Ann Costello, J.J. Hornblass, Amy Marcus, Glenn Wolfson

NEWS EXECUTIVE, $500 or more
Anonymous, David Dunlap, Bobby Fieseler, Mary Fisher, Hana Fuchs, Michael Jacobs

RIGHTS AND PERMISSIONS

"Homosexuals Confronting a Time of Change," "Citing Stress, F.D.A. Aide Wants Out," "AIDS Test," "On the Book-Signing Circuit with Magic Johnson; Call Him Earvin: 'I Can't Be Magic,'" "Covering AIDS And Living It: A Reporter's Testimony," "At Home With: Randy Shilts; Writing Against Time, Valiantly," "Whatever Happened to AIDS?," "A 50-State Ruling." Copyright © 1983, 1990, 1992, 1993 The New York Times Company. Reprinted by Permission.

ACT UP New York records, reprinted courtesy of Manuscripts and Archives Division. The New York Public Library. Astor, Lenox, and Tilden Foundations.

Excerpts from *Day One* broadcast and original research interviews © 1993 ABC News. Used by permission.

Excerpts from Michael Wilde's diary copyright © 2015 by Michael Wilde. Used by permission.

Cover photograph by Fred Conrad/*The New York Times*.

THE AUTHORS

Samuel G. Freedman is an award-winning journalist and educator. A columnist for *The New York Times* and a professor at Columbia University, and he is the author of the seven acclaimed books. He has been a finalist for the National Book Award and the Pulitzer Prize and has won the Helen Bernstein Award for Excellence in Journalism and the National Jewish Book Award. In 1997, the Society of Professional Journalists named Freedman the nation's outstanding journalism educator, and in 2012, he received Columbia University's Presidential Award for Outstanding Teaching.

Kerry Donahue is an experienced radio producer and the director of the radio program at Columbia University Graduate School of Journalism. Her work has been heard on PRI, PRX, NPR, WNYC, WBGO, and *Marketplace*. A former executive producer at WNYC, Kerry was part of the team that launched *The Takeaway* with John Hockenberry in 2008 and was the executive producer of *Pop & Politics with Farai Chideya*. She was an early podcast pioneer in her role as a producer of original content at Audible.com, a subsidiary of Amazon and the leading site for downloadable premium audio content.